My Game of Life

The Poetry and Essays
of
Edward Lull

Published by
High Tide Publications, Inc.
Deltaville, Virginia

Thank you for purchasing an authorized edition of *My Game of Life*.

High Tide's mission is to find, encourage, promote, and publish the work of authors. We are a small, woman-owned enterprise that is dedicated to the author over 50. When you buy an authorized copy, you help us to bring their work to you. When you honor copyright law by not reproducing or scanning any part (in any form) without our written permission, you enable us to support authors, publish their work, and bring it to you to enjoy. We thank you for supporting our authors.

High Tide Publications, Inc.
Deltaville, Virginia 23043
www.HighTidePublications.com

Illustrations and book design by FireBelliedFrog.com
Edited by Cindy L. Freeman

Printed in the United States of America

First Edition

Introduction

Having begun my writing career in my mid-sixties, I never ran short of life experiences to write about. Where younger writers face the dreaded "writer's block," the advice "Write about what you know," is often marginally helpful. It has worked for me. I have built this book around things I have done, ideas I have had, and emotions I felt strongly. It contains some of my favorite poems written in my first twenty years of writing as well as many relatively new unpublished works. The latter category includes responses to the devastating impact of losing my loving partner of more than sixty-three blessed years of marriage. Those wounds are indeed deep and lasting.

My years in the Emerson Society of Williamsburg produced numerous essays on a variety of topics. Several were written from research conducted on U.S. Navy history - a favorite topic of mine. Others included leadership training, risky childhood experiences, golfing exploits, and English language peculiarities. However, Part 4 of the book contains six essays detailing actual experiences I had as a Navy officer. I needed no notes to write these essays; the events are still permanently etched in my mind - fifty years later.

One advantage of taking up writing as a third career is that I fully intended to remain active and productive in retirement and I enjoy writing. So now, with the freedom to do so, I could put to use my leadership and management skills gained through 20 years as a Navy officer followed by 20 years of executive positions in business. Once into creative writing, I held leadership positions in the Poetry Society of Virginia, The Emerson Society of Williamsburg, St. Bede Catholic Church, and James City Poets. The participation in each has contributed immeasurably to the joys and fulfillment of my retirement goals.

I have known and worked with wonderful people throughout my life; I have love for all and ill will toward none. I am truly blessed.

I dedicate this book to my children who are always looking out for me:

Jeanne Lull Hopke — Edward W. Lull, Jr. — James M. Lull

What a team!

Edward W. Lull

Table of Contents

Part 3: Events, Opinions, Tales   63

Part 4: Navy Experiences (Essays)   **97**

Part 1: Experience

1.1 My Game of Life

My life till now has been much like a game
that's played in quarters, similar in length,
but different in objectives as you'll see.
Let's lay out eighty-seven years this way:

In quarter one my focus was to learn,
so EDUCATION was the theme throughout.
From parents, teachers, and professors I
prepared myself for quarter number two. (23 years)

Beginning naval SERVICE while at war,
I found myself well-suited to the life.
My yearn for travel was fulfilled these years
but love of family said, "It's time to go." (21 years)

My move into the BUSINESS world was not
as seamless as I hoped that it would be.
Although it did provide for family needs,
I missed the changing scenes of Navy life. (21 years)

RETIREMENT opened up another world
as writing brought creative forces and
a satisfaction that had been asleep.
Both poetry and prose absorbed my days. (21 years)

When illnesses and aging took their toll
and threatened termination of my game,
I phased down my activities, received
good care; my game went into OVERTIME.

So now I find myself with no good charts
to navigate this wide transition sea
I must rely on all that I have learned
to reach that distant shore called destiny. (To be determined)

1.2 Mid-Winter Encounter

Loose driveway stones crackled under tires
as I approached my garage,
biting cold and dark as tar.
High beams illuminated the garage door
and newly trimmed vitex bush.
My vision fastened
on the bulky object on branch stubs,
at eye level and motionless.
It was an owl, wings folded,
unruffled by my presence
or by being on stage, in the spotlight,
surrounded by blackness.

Emerging from the car, I stood still,
exchanging stares with this regal creature.
A large head, flat face with glistening eyes
and short, hooked beak,
sat atop a hawk-sized body
with speckled brown feathers.
Although I have heard owls at night,
I had never seen one up close.
I stood a dozen feet away, like a statue,
my sense of awe growing.
Suddenly his head swivelled,
as if on a well-oiled bearing.
Nothing seen, he resumed his curious gaze.
What thoughts danced behind those blazing eyes?
What instincts assured him I was no threat?

This marvelous bird remained placid,
until garage door creaking broke the spell,
disturbing the equilibrium of the encounter.
I experienced a strange sadness
when, with a whirr of waving wings,
he vanished into the night.

1.3 The Ballad of Deliverance
or
Dropping Off a Daughter at College

"Sunny, hot, and humid" blared
the radio upstairs.
This August date I hardly cared,
so wrapped up in my prayers.

The year - a long, long time ago,
our daughter was, at last,
packing for the trip, you know,
the time has gone so fast.

Acceptance at her school of choice
seemed wonderful in June;
I hardly think I shall rejoice
this summer afternoon.

A loaded car; it's time to go,
for Williamsburg we're bound.
The conversation seemed to flow,
but we were tightly wound.

The temperature was ninety-four
when we reached Barrett Hall.
"I'll carry stuff, you get the door."
"Be careful not to fall."

Unloading took an hour plus,
the sweat was flowing free.
'Twas then the roommates greeted us;
I was a sight to see.

Parents talked and roommates shared;
"That one's an extrovert."
We wondered if she were prepared;
my head began to hurt.

One roommate asked, "What's your I.Q.?"
My stomach churned a bit.
The time to leave had come, I knew,
there's no avoiding it.

Goodbyes are hard and always lead
to tears and trite expression.
We cannot bring the depth we need
to offset the depression.

We drove off, left our pride, our joy,
defenseless, as it were.
"I hope you saw that dark-haired boy,
the way he looked at her."

My wife was silent then for good,
a tear leaked from her eye.
We knew we'd done the best we could;
she'd earned her wings to fly.

1.4 A Special Christmas

The festive lights of Christmas
broke the wall of darkness
as we arrived at the appointed hour.
The three of us were shown in,
ushered through a long hallway,
and into the dimly lit chapel.
As we entered our pew, we knelt,
said brief prayers, exchanged glances,
said nothing.

Three Naval officers, submariners,
were about to share the solemn
celebration of Midnight Mass
with the royal couple, in the palace
of the principality of Monaco.
Our invitations had been delivered as
our submarine moored in the harbor
days before.

Prince Rainier and Princess Grace entered the chapel,
nodded to their guests, then knelt in their pew.
I have attended Masses in many beautiful
churches and cathedrals, but this celebration
of The Feast of the Nativity in a relatively
simple chapel had the aura of welcoming,
fitting for the birth being commemorated.

Supper and gift-giving with the royal couple
and a few of their close friends followed Mass.
After a delightful meal and stimulating conversation,
Princess Grace went to the royally decorated tree
and began presenting gifts to her guests.
My gift was a silk tie from Simpson of Piccadilly
that has seldom left its place on my tie-rack
in the fifty years since I received it.

While other members of our crew were
enjoying the bright lights and activities
of Monte Carlo, I was experiencing
a quiet Christmas Eve to remember
for a lifetime.

1.5 The Indigo Bunting

Sitting on the porch at the "home,"
trying to make conversation
with my dad was not working.
His far-off gaze showed
little interest in my babbling
about nothing in particular.

His rocker just six feet from mine,
but our minds were worlds apart.
His was enveloped in a confusing
state of nothingness, inescapable,
and impossible for me to penetrate.

A male cardinal flew by and perched
on a wire across the street. My mind
took me back many years to a trip
from Greenwich to Troy where my dad
and I would do some painting
in a house that would soon be our home.

Our car was cruising at fifty
when Dad hit the brakes and
guided the car off the side of the road.
"Get out," he commanded, and
moved quickly to the rear of the car.
He pointed to a bird on a telephone
wire across the street. "You won't
see many of those in this area;
it's an indigo bunting."

While driving, he spotted a bird on a wire,
identified it, rare though it was,
and felt he should stop the car
to point out to his teen-age son
a sight he had not seen before;
that defined my dad in earlier days.

As we were leaving the home, a male nurse
came on the porch from inside.
He asked, "Richard, do you know
who visited you today?"
Dad looked confused, and mumbled,
"Nobody."

1.6 The Day the Skinny Lab Died

Electrical engineering, a subject area we called Skinny,
was not my strong suit at the Academy.
I struggled with it academically,
had to work hard just to pass.

The final hurdle to clear was
a practical exam called the Skinny Lab.
When each section arrived at the lab,
students would be handed a slip of paper
with an individual assignment on it.
We would go to our stations,
wire up whatever our individual assignment was,
apply the power, and pray that it ran.

*   *   *   *   *   *   *

Exam eve, I studied with a few classmates,
reviewing a half-dozen or so possibilities
that our assignment could be. The final one
I studied was, perhaps, the easiest -
a shunt-wound motor. I acknowledged
that my three greatest fears were:
spiders, snakes, and 250 volts.
Tomorrow, the last would be first.

*   *   *   *   *   *   *

As I entered the lab the next morning,
the professor handed me the dreaded assignment slip.
Acting cool, I casually glanced at it and saw
Shunt-Wound Motor. Inwardly, my confidence
surged. I went to my station and surveyed
the equipment at my disposal. Go slow,
I told myself, remembering that I was dealing with
250 volts.

By the time I completed my wiring,
many of my smarter classmates had
completed their projects, and the lab
was filled with the music of dozens
of whirring motors and generators.
Ready to add my motor to the chorus,
I confidently thrust my power lead into
the 250-volt bus in the floor. A small
lightning bolt leaped from the bus.

The symphony went: **rrrrrrr**rrr - then silence.
The lights went out; the profs ran
from station to station to locate the problem,
but everyone's exam was over.
I had blown the building's main circuit breaker.

*　　*　　*　　*　　*　　*　　*

Fifty-some years later I was playing golf
with another Academy alum about twenty
years younger than I, when this came to my mind.
I told him the story, and as I was finishing
he looked at me with a huge grin.
"So you're the one! When I went through
that lab, the profs were still telling the story.
All midshipmen have heard it."
"Yep" I said, "I'm the one who did it."

Later I was thinking that those
who came after me never knew:
I was selected to represent my classmates
on the Brigade Honor Committee;
led my company cross-country team;
quarterbacked the company touch football team;
pitched for the company softball team;
was the final set 11th Company Commander.
But they had all learned about
the day the skinny lab died.
Walking down the 18th fairway, my stride
took on a bit of a swagger; I thought,
I am a legend.

1.7 To My Granddaughter
(on beginning her college adventure)
A Rubáiyát

Your cruise from Here to There will be
across the wide Transition Sea.
With visibility not clear
your future has no guarantee.

Your navigation tools, my dear,
were yours before you left from Here.
To find them all you must prevail
and force solutions to appear.

When storms arise with wind and hail,
you'll steer your ship around the gale.
The links from shore remain your source
of strength and they will never fail.

If ever winds have such a force
they try to blow your ship off course,
remember where your anchors are;
you're ethics will avoid remorse.

So know your journey's not too far
and don't lose sight of that bright star.
Enjoy the trip to your degree;
it's chapter one of your memoir.

1.8 To Face the Night
(A Villanelle)

I go, not willingly, to face the night.
Although the joys of living still are strong,
my limitations soon will dim the light.

My friends and loved ones, beacons shining bright,
but pain and illness render days too long.
I go, not willingly, to face the night.

I never shall complain about my plight;
life has been kind and little has gone wrong,
but limitations soon will dim the light.

No problems in my life I couldn't fight;
no place I've been where I did not belong.
I go, not willingly, to face the night.

If I've offended any, I'm contrite.
There are no grudges that I would prolong,
but limitations soon will dim the light.

My code has been: just do what I think right,
so sadness will not fill my evensong.
I go, not willingly, to face the night;
my limitations soon will dim the light.

1.9 Nature's Oldest Gift

From time to time, my wife and I
heard noise from our garage.
We thought some critter just might try
to make our home his lodge.

Recalling finding on the floor
things that had been on shelves.
They had, we ascertained for sure,
not fallen by themselves.

So now we had a mystery;
who is this resident?
What type of tenant might he be?
We know he pays no rent.

Next day we took a careful look
upstairs as well as down.
Behind a box we found his nook;
he ran; his fur dark brown.

His pointy face and rat-like tail
identified his breed.
To catch him certainly would fail,
despite his lack of speed.

Opossums like to be alone
so captured, he would fight.
To let him stay, I'd not condone;
let's hope he's not too bright.

I scattered granules of fox scent
around the entryways,
and places where we knew he went
I put mothball sachets.

I hope these simple steps will show
he's not a welcome guest.
His is an ancient breed, although
to me, he's just a pest.

As time goes on the news is good
he's not been in his box.
If he shows up, and he well could,
we may just hire a fox...
or not.

1.10 Lasting Friendships

"Who were some of your close friends,
not family?" the interviewer asked.

"Bob, my roommate at the Academy
for three years, and I shared many
of our expectations and concerns
about the military life we would soon
undertake. His fiancée, Marge, and
my fiancée became quite close:
he was best man at our wedding.

"Mac, also a midshipman, and Joyce
often double dated with Evelyn and me.
Our first duty stations were in the same
division of destroyers in San Diego.
Our paths crossed many times during
our Navy careers - and beyond.

"Dick and Charlene lived in the apartment
above ours in Coronado; both couples
had first children there. We shared the joys
and demands of babies. While I was on a
six-month deployment, Dick taught Evelyn
to drive, and she was a life-time good driver.

"Richard and I were shipmates on my first submarine; he provided great assistance and training for me to earn my dolphins.
We were both old movie buffs and a tough bridge team. Richard and Phyllis became very close friends with us."

"Are these folks still close friends?"

"I still write real Christmas cards.
As I wrote cards to Marge, Joyce, Charlene, and Phyllis, I realized that I was living what each of them had experienced: all four are widows."

"So you are the last man standing; you must feel quite lucky."
"Not really, 'lucky' applies to winning the football pool, but not to the game of life!"

1.11 God's Call

The sun rose with a special glow that day,
the long anticipated time had passed.
And now my love had painful work to do,
a task she undertook with verve and grace...
The time had come!

Enveloped by a wave of joyous thoughts,
we dreamt about the things that were to be:
the wonders of the life that lay ahead.
Our first born child - a son - a gift from God...
And he was here!

The second day the clouds had dimmed the glow,
our happiness was tempered with concern.
But hopeful parents never dream the worst,
we knew our little son could make it through...
Then he was gone!

He never knew his mother's loving touch,
he never saw the beauty of the sky.
How could a little life be ended thus?
And we be left behind to wonder why...
We felt alone!

The pain of loss can leave eternal scars,
we never even brought him to our home.
But years and wisdom helped us understand:
God's plan for him was different from our own...
And he is home!

1.12 On My Mother's Passing

We spoke in hushed and muted tones,
disjointed thoughts about the past.
Our efforts to block out the truth
through aimless conversation failed.

The moans from upstairs pierced the night
and jarred us into silent prayer.
Dear Lord, her whole life has been Yours;
please take her now and give her peace.

A sturdy woman, small but strong,
unflagging and fulfilling faith
defined her life. She knew hard times,
and wealth and ease not hers to keep.

Just months ago - it seems like years,
her cancer struck and spread like flames.
First in her lungs and then her brain;
her sentence harsh with no appeal.

Accepting fate, as was her way,
with grace that made her life so blessed.
This son could not be so benign,
his faith felt doubts as none before.

The torment of the night went on;
her cries of agony were knives
thrust coarsely in my chest.
Dear Lord, what more must she endure?

At last the drugs took full effect;
she fell into relaxed repose.
Her loving heart was also strong,
delaying this, her voyage home.

My mother didn't die that night;
she fought for life, but won just days.
She was prepared to meet her Lord,
and died with courage as she lived.

1.13 A Blessed Journey

To Evelyn:

A windy, wintry day in '53
we walked above the rocks on Severn's shore.
I knew commitment time was here - and we
agreed to share our lives forevermore.

On June the fourth of 1955
we said our solemn vows and thus began
a blessed journey on that joyful road
of love between a woman and a man.

The Navy kept us moving place-to-place,
and sometimes caused us lengthy times apart.
We learned the hurt of separation was
a test to the devotion of the heart.

Despite the painful loss of our first son,
our children came and claimed their share of love.
They soon became the focus of our lives;
they were most welcome gifts from God above.

In just one blink they all grew up and left
and each pursued the challenge of career.
But then in just two blinks the grandkids came;
a whole new outlet for our love was here.

And now another generation joins
as six great-grands have further blest our lives.
Our home becomes the place of great delight
each year when time for giving thanks arrives.

Each anniversary we turn the page
as we have done for sixty-three great years.
However, this time everything would change;
the page is blank except for stain of tears.

On looking back we could be justly proud
that every single vow we took, we meant.
Commitment packed with love will never break;
to me, I know that you were heaven-sent.
With all my love, Ed

1.14 Eventide Bereavement

As darkness shrouds my lonely life again
and waves of sadness reach into my soul,
my broken heart views loss as its domain
and wonders if it ever can be whole.

My active life was always wrapped in her;
I gloried in the thought that she was mine.
Our silent times together - now a blur;
I sipped her presence like the finest wine.

The future, always bright, engulfed in fog,
those things that brought us joy now pass me by.
Our children join in prayerful dialogue;
rebuilding may just be a goal too high.

My inner self refuses to retire;
new challenges I don't expect to start.
So I'll continue what life may require;
but understand what's missing in my heart.

1.15 The Unguarded Moment

We've heard the story many times;
mother and child, walking hand-in-hand,
mother lets go of child in a moment of distraction.
In an instant - child is gone.
Her child - her baby -
how could she be so careless?

On hole number thirteen, my nemesis,
on the Heath of Black, a fair drive
followed by an excellent 7-iron lay-up shot,
left me a wedge from the green.
I was going around the water, not over it.
You won't defeat me this time, I thought.
However, my lob-wedge failed to lob - it sculled,
sending my white ball skittering
across the dormant Bermuda grass,
quickly out of my short-sighted vision.

Just short of the green, pulling my push-cart
between the bunker and the pond bank,
I did not spot my ball where I expected
to encounter it. Could it have kicked left
into the sand? Releasing my cart, I took
one step left to peek into the bunker.
The sound of club-heads clinking together
caused me to spin around to see
my cart, bag, and clubs careening
down the bank toward the pond.
I, normally the one to step forward at crisis time,
stood motionless, mouth agape,
like a helpless doofus, and watched
as my golfing essentials took one final bounce,
and belly-flopped into the pond.

As the cart slid beneath the water,
only part of one wheel remained
above the surface - gasping for air.
A golfing partner, whom I call hero-man,
said, "I can get it," and removed his shoes and socks.
Stepping gingerly into the frigid water
that had a layer of ice five days earlier,
he began the retrieval operation
that took more than ten foot-numbing minutes.

"Is that everything?" hero-man asked,
I replied, hesitatingly, "all but my 7-iron."
Back in he went and retrieved the recalcitrant club.
Miraculously, nothing was lost; the only casualty
was a water-logged antiquated cell phone.

After dumping the water from the many pockets,
I opted to do what every avid golfer would do:
continue the round.
I announced that I would drop on the bank
where my ball had apparently gone
into the water (with my cart and bag in cold pursuit).
"Why?" hero-man called. "You're up here."
He pointed to a prim white spheroid, the only
dry piece of golf equipment I owned, sitting
twenty feet from the pin. At my creative best,
I replied, "Well I'll be damned!"

The next time I read about a mother's
unguarded moment with a child,
I shall show considerable compassion.
Were I there, I'd console her with,
"Take heart - have faith - you are not to blame,"
and, (visualizing my ball
sitting high and dry on the green)
"remember, this is just a metaphor."

1.16 The Love-Hate Game

My love for the golf course I don't understand.
I spend so much time in the woods and in sand.
I see great improvement each time on the range,
but then when I play my score just doesn't change.

No matter what part of my game that goes well,
a leveling force casts its score-killing spell.
When hitting my driver with all sorts of power,
my chipping goes nowhere - my putting goes sour.

I think that my partners just take me along
to be an example of what can go wrong.
My handicap should let me win on occasion,
but I've yet to locate that winning equation.

*   *   *   *   *   *   *

Wow! Look at that drive, it's so long and so straight;
my love for this game I cannot overstate.

1.17 The Christmas Party

As a member of the submarine *Tench*,
we were experiencing an early cold winter.
I was very pleased to receive
an invitation to a Christmas party.

My boss was the sub's captain;
his boss was the division commander;
his boss was the squadron commander,
a senior captain, aspiring to flag rank.
The squadron commander invited us.

It was a dress-up, catered affair,
with delightful heavy hors d'oeuvres,
and various beverages, including
a well-spiked egg nog -
a happy way to open the season.

We didn't want to overstay, so
as the party began to wind down,
we eased toward the front door,
where our hostess was stationed.
Evelyn said, "Thank you so much,
the egg log was denicious"
I followed that with, "We had
a wonderful time, Virginia."

As we got out on the cold sidewalk,
Evelyn asked, "Did I just say
the egg log was denicious?"
"Yes, you did."
"Did you say good-bye to Virginia?"
"Certainly."
"Her name is Carolyn."

We walked on in silence for a while.
"We probably won't be invited
back next year, will we?"
"Probably not."

1.18 Incomplete Spring

Tiny waves, sparkling in Long Island sun,
shushed across the sand.
Tepid breezes carried scents of the new-born season.
Manly oaks ignored
the chartreuse doilies emerging
from their barren boughs. Golden-glow forsythia
along the parkway waved a welcome
as I headed toward the "home."
Everything around me proclaimed
spring's grand awakening -

except my dad.

Whether the alcohol or the accident carved
that gaping hole in his memory I didn't know.
Reluctantly I had acknowledged that I was in the section
that was gone forever.
Although friendly and lucid as we conversed,
I was just a visitor;
he did not know me as his son.
Our visit went well; he enjoyed my company.
On a branch beyond the open window,
a Baltimore oriole warbled its joyful-season song.
My dad, a devoted lover of tree and sea, bird and flower,
didn't notice.

1.19 Read The Label

I recently bought a ten-dollar,
hand-held, digital stop watch;
it was "Made in China."

I marveled at the secure packaging
of thick cardboard and heavy-duty plastic.
Usually, if there are no instructions
on how to defeat the bullet-proof
outer garments, I find and attack
a weak point. There were none.
With sharp scissors and considerable
hand strength I cut through the outer
wall and freed the enslaved watch.

I noticed two paragraphs of fine print
on the cardboard package. The first,
in caps and bold face said "WARNING:
BE VIGILANT AT ALL TIMES. Keep
the product clean and visible to others
at all times." I laid the watch gently
on the table, wondering if I would need
a license to put the watch in my pocket.

The second paragraph was headed Caution:
The first sentence read: "Do not open."
Aha - now I understand the packaging
philosophy. The second sentence said:
"Do not dispose of product into fire."
Okay, I can live with that. Next it warned:
"May short circuit, explode or leak."
Now I won't put it in my pocket!
The final significant caution I promise
to abide by. It read:
"Do not swallow."

I hope the watch works well,
but honestly, the labels alone
were worth $9.95.

1.20 Witness to the Crime

The brilliant sun at summer's peak
warmed my shoulders as I walked
through field and forest.
Nature was at peace,
my imagination at rest.
Approaching home, I stepped
onto the road, mind wandering.

Suddenly I spotted a silent,
motionless bird on the road,
twenty feet directly in front of me,
wings spread, seemingly dead
or injured. I froze on the spot;
by coloring and size, I recognized
a marsh hawk. This creature
is seldom a victim.

After staring briefly, I ventured
a step or two toward this bird of prey.
With one motion, he rose to full height,
sprang upward with a powerful leap,
flapped strong, broad wings,
and became airborne. Then I saw,
dangling from his talons,
a lifeless adult squirrel.

Reconstructing the scene in my mind,
I pictured the furry fellow crossing the road,
unaware of imminent danger.
The silent predator swooped down,
grasping his unsuspecting prey,
and spreading his wings
to achieve privacy. His lethal talons
swiftly completed the job.
I was just an accidental witness
to a sordid act of nature.

Later, while enjoying a chicken dinner,
I mused about the hidden side of civilization
compared to the openness of nature.
The hawk was hungry; he used his skill to kill.
For my meal, I paid for the execution.

1.21 Unexpected Loss

"Better wrap that up, Pat's on in five."
Completion of my letter could wait;
I rose from my computer, went downstairs.
She was in her chair; I reclined in mine.

Pat and Vanna entertained us both,
then Alex had his time to test our skill.
We used commercial time to brief our day
and then exchange whatever either wished.

My wife and I had followed this routine
at home for most of our retirement years.
There were a couple other shows we liked,
but they were on at inconvenient times.

*   *   *   *   *   *   *

Last week a friend asked, "Did you see that guy
who won a million dollars on the 'Wheel?'"
I answered "No" but then gave it some thought.
When was the last time I had watched that show?

Those game shows just had never crossed my mind;
I realized I had not watched them alone.
My mind began to sort through what was lost;
apparently the shows were not the draw.

It's not a piece of life that I had put in place;
in time, I'm sure some others will appear.
They told me life would never be the same;
some wounds are just too deep to fully heal.

1.22 New Worlds

Which way to go and where to turn,
I've truly lost my way.
The things I built my life around
are fading day by day.

> When sadness tries to take command
> One must dig deep and make a stand.

My ethics and my inner self
are what they've always been,
My goals of yore, alive no more,
I need a race to win.

> When sadness tries to take command
> One must dig deep and make a stand.

The years have taken much of life
that brought me to this place.
My partner's gone, I thrive alone;
old steps I can't retrace.

> When sadness tries to take command
> One must dig deep and make a stand.

If some day hence my strength returns
with challenges anew,
I'll regain purpose that brings joy,
new worlds I may pursue.

> When sadness tries to take command
> One must dig deep and make a stand.

1.23 Love and Peace

She was my partner all those years,
a team that I was justly proud.
Our love was real as were my tears;
it's hard to say "she's gone" out loud.

When grieving for a loss, recall
that love brings joy and peace to all.

They say that life goes on, of course,
but mine can never be the same.
For happiness she was my source,
each day since when she took my name.

When grieving for a loss, recall
that love brings joy and peace to all.

If every man could be so blest
as I have been to share this love,
then hate would always be repressed
for peace and love go hand-in-glove.

When grieving for a loss, recall
that love brings joy and peace to all.

Part 2: Special Days

2.1 Where Giants Walked
(*An Independence Day* walk on
Duke of Gloucester Street, Colonial Williamsburg)

A stroll on this historic street provokes
an awesome sense that here they met and talked.
The sunlight filters through majestic oaks
as reverently I walk where giants walked.

We call them patriots of times long gone;
Virginians all, they shared a common dream.
Their forebears set a standard whereupon
the sons made freedom their enduring theme.

The Capital from sixteen ninety nine,
for eighty years through peace and joy and fear;
this city - Williamsburg - remained a shrine
of liberty, evolving year by year.

As foreign rule increasingly inflamed
the spark of revolutionary thought,
Virginia's leaders forcefully proclaimed
that they would not be bullied nor be bought.

When Jefferson and Henry, Mason, Bland,
and Washington; the Randolphs and the Lees;
and Harrison and Braxton were on hand,
the City hosted greatness: freedom's keys.

Resounding oratory filled the air,
the Capitol, intense with fervent sound.
Debate resumed at Raleigh's Tavern where
the seeds of freedom fell on fertile ground.

The risks were high, but passion for their goal
defeated fear that lesser men sustained.
They formed a Union with both heart and soul,
a gallant victory that brave men gained.

This sojourn down colonial promenade
recalls for me how these men earned renown:
commitment to their cause and faith in God,
where giants walked - in Williamsburg - their town.

2.2 The Final Honor
A Memorial Day Sonnet

Moist fresh-mown grass disturbed by naked earth
contrasts the beauty where fall flowers bloomed.
No standard headstone yet to mark the berth
where loyal teenage soldier is entombed.

The scene of caisson towed by ambling horse
on winding paths within this honored place
repeats itself too often in the course
of honoring these lives too soon erased.

These are not aged veterans who, at last,
are shown respect long due for sacrifice.
They are our proud young soldiers who were cast
in drama where they paid war's highest price.

Though for their bravery we can't repay,
we honor and salute them on this day,

2.3 Lest We Forget
Armed Forces Day

Dogwood trees and buttercups
bring the land to life.
Springtime's glory never fails
Brandywine's North Creek.
Forebears gave their lives.   *Revolutionary War*

Lawrence sailed on troubled seas
into the bloody fray.
"Don't give up the ship," he cried,
"Fight her till she sinks."
And then he died.   *War of 1812*

Tassels tossed by gentle winds,
corn stalks rich with fruit;
dusty road and stony bridge
at Antietam Creek.
Soldiers fell en masse.   *Civil War*

"Charge!" he ordered, charge they did,
straight up San Juan Hill.
Emotions high in man and horse,
ignoring heat, they fought.
Some did not return.   *Spanish American War*

Morning mist engulfs the trees,
underbrush deep green;
later sunbeams burn their paths
into Belleau Wood.
Many never left.   *World War I*

Lush green foliage all around,
trees with vines and fruit.
Jungle sounds envelop all;
tranquil isle, Bataan.
Brave men's final march.   *World War II - Pacific*

Rolling hills with farmland plots,
friendly, happy folks.
Peaceful scene for one to paint,
near the town Bastogne.
"Nuts" to giving up.   *World War II - Europe*

Rocky crags peer through the drifts,
chill winds keep them bare.
White and black and shaded grays;
hues at Pork Chop Hill.
Peace talks stalled, they froze.   *Korea*

Graceful ferns sway with the breeze,
monsoon rains ensue.
Multi-colored plants abound;
beauty at Khe Sanh.
Brothers died alone.   *Vietnam*

Swirling winds make hot sand sting,
impeding an attack.
Intense fight, incessant heat:
conditions in Iraq.
Friends blown to bits.   *Iraq and Afghanistan*

Freedom's price - a heavy toll;
life is ours to spend.
Dying for one's country is
dying for a friend.
Lest we forget!

2.4 To Those Who Gave
Veterans Day

They marched, they flew, they sailed, they rode
away to do their country's work.
The ones they loved remained behind
with little but the clouds of doubt.

They were not heroes when they left
and knew not where their paths would lead.
Bravado was the outer shell;
uncertainty was there within.

Some went to war on thick-soled boots,
to face a foe they never knew.
They killed because they had no choice,
or died because they thought they did.

Some took their war into the sky,
with weapons awesome to behold.
Their skill and daring made us proud,
and yet, some still went down in flames.

Some chose the sea to do their work,
in mighty ships with wide-mouthed guns
and hulls of steel with armor plate;
but many never made it back.

When all was done those left came home,
but their return was bittersweet.
Reunions with their loved ones sweet,
yet bitter scars of war remained.

They were not heroes when they left,
nor do they think they're heroes now.
Bravado gone, they aged so much;
their lives will never be the same.

As years go by and thoughts of war
are far from central to our lives,
we owe a debt too great to pay,
except for thanks to those who gave.

2.5 Called to Serve
Patriots Day

It wasn't called a war, but he was called to serve.
His sweetheart saw him off - a soldier far too soon.
A high school grad last spring, he knew what he would do.
The farm would be his life; he'd call the land his own.

This interruption just delayed his lifetime plans.
He'd do his bit and then return to Georgia's soil.
He knew that General Doug would turn this thing around
and get the boys like him back to the lives they left.

To infantry he went - a grunt - as he was called.
His training - very brief - a ship then took him west.
Korea's ice and snow were half a world away
from Georgia's warming sun and from the life he knew.

Realities of war were closing on him fast;
his peaceful world would change this bitter day.
His company called to spearhead an attack.
The sickness in his gut foretold what he must face.

His squad on the point; they crawled through snow and mud.
The cold he never felt as bullets rained around.
He passed a fallen foe and checked for signs of life.
But suddenly his thigh was struck - and he went down.

He did his best to stop the blood from flowing free.
Where are the medics? Now he knew he needed help;
the others on the ground nearby were still and cold.
The battle had moved on; he felt he was alone.

He called for help, but found his voice was getting weak;
perhaps some rest would help restore his sapping strength.
His pain had eased somewhat, the snow a restful bed.
He said his evening prayers - and drifted off to sleep.

- - - - - - - - - - - - - - - - -

They sent his casket home; no bands nor fanfare there;
no gold star to display; no closure for the pain.
While politicians talked, he gave his country all;
It wasn't called a war - but he was called to die.

2.6 Symbol of Glory
Flag Day

We pledge allegiance to our flag
and fly it high across the land.
To withstand trials throughout the years,
it stands for something great and grand.

This banner born in troubled times
not quite a year from when brave men
stood firm together to proclaim
their freedom with a stroke of pen.

Red, white, and blue the colors were;
with red the strength and courage hue;
integrity and virtue: white;
stability and justice: blue.

Immortalized by brilliant stripes
those colonies that fought the war.
Each colony and then each state
that joined the Union earned a star.

From Valley Forge to Fort McHenry,
Fredericksburg to San Juan Hill,
Americans have fought and died,
their obligations to fulfill.

From Argonne Forest to Bastogne
and Suribachi to Inchon,
this flag of destiny gave strength
to urge the weary warriors on.

The magic of this standard lives
within the hearts of countrymen
who understand that freedom's cost
is high, and will be paid again.

So June fourteen we set aside
one day per year to recognize
our flag - and all for which it stands:
ideals this banner sanctifies.

2.7 King of Equality
Martin Luther King Day

His legacy was Georgia born,
and preaching was his call.
His message was a simple one:
equality for all.

At first his voice was heard by just
the faithful of his flock.
Was equal rights for all the key
to racial bonds unlock?

He led the marches through the South
for justice to prevail.
But often keepers of the law
put Martin King in jail.

Despite indignities he faced,
he took them all in stride
and made his plea for freedom heard;
his fame spread nationwide.

His peaceful coexistence text
became a movement's theme.
Could races live in harmony?
That quest - his lifelong dream.

Though change proved hard for some to face
the vision he would build.
So when a bigot took his life,
his dream was unfulfilled.

But Martin Luther King's life work
continues to this day.
Inequities and biased views
have never gone away.

2.8 The Ballad of Harry S.
Presidents' Day

He fought the war to end all wars,
a captain at the end.
The loyal men of Batt'ry D
would always call him friend.
A business man - that he was not;
the clothes store doomed to fail.
But when he turned to politics,
old Harry made the sale.

A judge in Jackson County, MO,
for eight successful years;
he learned the way to get things done
was just to use his ears
then tell the truth without concern
for risks to his career.
When Harry spoke folks knew they heard
his feelings, loud and clear.

They'd holler, "Harry, give 'em hell!"
And Harry gave 'em hell.

In nineteen hundred thirty-four,
his county work was done.
His senate bid caught fire, and he
was off to Washington.
The "powers" quickly learned that he
could not be bought or sold.
Each time they pushed a bit too far,
old Harry stopped 'em cold.

In '40, Harry ran again
with odds against him strong.
But politicking at his best
he proved the doubters wrong.
Now even FDR took note,
and when, in '44,
he needed a new running mate,
one loyal to the core.

They'd holler, "Harry, give 'em hell!"
And Harry gave 'em hell.

Just months into his new-found job,
death handed him the reins:
the outcome of the many battles
fought in his campaigns.
As President his role would change,
his country now to steer.
But Harry never changed his style;
he said: "The buck stops here!"

A war to win, a scary bomb,
a party badly split,
but Harry took them as they came
through skill, resolve, and wit.
Through awesome days he never lost
that comely down-home touch.
He had to deal with slippery folks
but didn't like it much.

They'd holler, "Harry, give 'em hell!"
And Harry gave 'em hell.

Joe Stalin gave him fits, but then
the airlift saved Berlin.
For Europe, Truman's Doctrine led
war's healing to begin.
His last campaign began when he
announced in '48.
The pundits - wrong again - he left
Tom Dewey at the gate.

McCarthy's "hunt," Korea's war,
then General Doug rebels.
The folks who tried to put him down
with guns wound up in cells.
When he left town, he went with grace;
he knew he'd done his best.
Plain spoken, short of stature, but
he soared above the rest!

They'd holler, "Harry, give 'em hell!"
And Harry gave 'em hell.

2.9 The Battle of Lake Erie
Navy Day

In early 1813, Oliver Hazard Perry sought a more active role in the war
and was reassigned from command of a gunboat flotilla in Newport to
direct the American naval effort on Lake Erie. At the time, there were no
naval forces on Lake Erie; the British controlled the lake. The American
land forces could not succeed in the west while the British controlled Lake
Erie.

*   *   *   *   *   *   *

An unencumbered line where sea met sky,
the lookout scanned about with watchful eye.
September morning's beauty went unseen,
for Captain Perry knew the day would bring
both challenges and pain of battle's sting;
his course was clear - let nothing intervene.

On deck he mused, *How would they meet the test?*
The times for building, training were compressed.
Just eight short months since Presque Isle first he saw,
no ships, no crew, a massive task at hand:
Secure Lake Erie; make it your command,
defeat the British; force them to withdraw.

*   *   *   *   *   *   *

A shipwright, Noah Brown, began to build
the ships with many workers barely skilled.
As wintry blasts slowed building more than planned,
throughout the backwoods camps the captain went
recruiting volunteers to complement
the corps of crew assigned to his command.

Captain Perry named his flagship for
James Lawrence, killed just three short months before.
A sky-blue battle banner raised with pride,
emblazoned with the hero's final phrase,
those words that made the fighting spirit blaze:
Don't give up the ship, he'd said - then died.

Mid-summer came, construction was complete;
the untrained crews were drilled in August heat.
Two brigs with twenty guns, and smaller craft
comprised the fleet; with Lawrence in the lead,
Niagra close behind with matching speed;
remaining smaller ships fell in abaft.

Among the crew was Perry's brother James,
a midshipman who shared his lofty aims.
Though pleased to have the youth beside him now,
the captain feared in battles to arise,
he might be forced to witness James' demise,
but midshipmen must pass this test somehow.

*   *   *   *   *   *   *

The British squadron on Lake Erie bore
its long-range guns aboard six men-of-war.
One-armed Robert Barclay was in charge,
(he'd been among Lord Nelson's retinue)
Detroit his flagship, battle-tested crew.
Captain Perry's task was looming large.

*   *   *   *   *   *   *

The battle group sailed west, the hunt began;
for days the lack of wind delayed their plan.
Despite increasing sail, the pace was slow.
Though boredom seized the crew, this soon would change
whenever British ships would come in range.
The early morning silence broke, *Sail Ho*!

The flagship *Lawrence*, leading, turned to close
and sorted through the foe to juxtapose.
Above the midday breeze, a fateful sound
when "Rule Britannia" drifted from *Detroit*.
This motivated Perry to exploit
his battle skills, his rival to confound.

As Perry moved his ship through heavy fire
while standing tall, his forces to inspire,
maneuvering to bring *Detroit* abeam.
With gun-for-gun and man-for-man they fought,
with brave men dying under the onslaught.
Their boldness, strength, and courage were the theme.

The boom - boom - boom of cannon numbed the ear,
while acrid smell of smoke made nostrils sear;
hot powder's stinging lashes singed the face.
The sight of fallen comrades on the deck,
with gaping wounds to body, head, and neck
made hardened warriors cringe without disgrace.

The smoke of battle crept across the lake
at gunwale level, putrid and opaque;
each breath brought bitter pungent tang to taste.
But battle on they did as best they could,
their numbers dwindled, but they understood
no greater test had any crewman faced.

Within two hours, only twenty stood,
while eighty-three stout hearts were stopped for good.
When *Lawrence* had its final gun destroyed,
the captain, brother James, plus four men more
rowed on to board *Niagara* to restore
their leader to a ship to be deployed.

Niagara sailed into the fray with verve,
its cheering crew held nothing in reserve.
Their weary foe now short of man and gun;
with Perry's hard-fought vict'ry all but sealed,
the badly wounded Barclay forced to yield,
the battle ended; Perry's mission done.

When all the captured ships had been secured,
and his small fleet still floating, safely moored,
the captain penned his terse report that said:
"We have met the enemy," he wrote
"and they are ours. Two ships, two brigs," (his note
went on) *"one schooner, and one sloop"* (it read).

As Captain Perry praised his gallant men,
he comforted the wounded once again.
Though death had taken many of his crew,
he thanked the Lord his brother was alive.
The boy, but twelve, was lucky to survive.
He smiled at James and said, *"We've much to do!"*

*   *   *   *   *   *   *

Oliver Hazard Perry's victory enabled the American military to regain
control of the northwest. His brief message to General William Henry
Harrison became as famous in navy annals as his battle flag. The battle
was the only instance in British naval history where an entire squadron
was surrendered. After the war, in 1819, while on a diplomatic mission
in South America for President Monroe, Oliver Hazard Perry contracted
yellow fever and died at age thirty-four.

2.10 When Christ Was Born
Christmas Day

As dawn crept in like other days,
no blast from fanfare horn.
On verdant hills the sheep could graze,
that day when Christ was born.

When shepherds heard the angels sing
it was a blessed morn.
They wondered what their God would bring
that day when Christ was born.

The magi from the East observed
the star that would forewarn
that something great had just occurred,
that day when Christ was born.

Just Mary knew that she had done
the duty she had sworn
to bring into the world God's son,
that day when Christ was born.

Who knew that one day He would face
the pain of public scorn?
But now His mother smiled with grace,
that day when Christ was born.

Millennia have passed, and yet
our homes we still adorn
to celebrate and not forget
that day when Christ was born.

As choirs sing and church bells ring
we welcome our new King.
Let all of heaven's angels sing
to welcome Christ the King.

2.11 Day of Infamy
Pearl Harbor Day

This day began much like the Sundays past;
few dreamt the nightmare soon to change their lives.
An ugly war had raged for two plus years;
Hawaii, though, was half a world away.

Oahu was a hub of naval might
with battleships and carriers and planes
of many types. But in the early hours
this peaceful morning, Pearl Harbor was asleep.

December 7, 1941,
at five till eight, the air attack began.
Initial waves dive bombed and strafed the planes
tied down at all five military fields.

Torpedo planes and bombers then attacked
the battleships and others moored around
Ford Islands row. Most battleships took hits
by bombs, torpedoes, plus the strafing runs.

The greatest single loss occurred when one
of five bomb hits on *Arizona* struck
a magazine that triggered towers of fire
and smoke, and ripped this massive ship apart.

Then *Arizona* sank, all hands aboard.
Of all American fatalities
occurring on this devastating day,
half of them were *Arizona's* crew.

The second wave of bombers added death,
destruction, and more chaos to the scene.
Ships did their best to man their guns and fight,
but moored in port, attackers had the edge.

When finally its boilers came online,
Nevada slowly backed out of its slip
to try to make a run for open sea.
The enemy had hoped for such a move.

If any major ship got underway,
attackers would all focus on that ship.
To sink it in the channel would abort
escape attempts by any other ships.

Though badly hurt from hits by many bombs,
Nevada slowly moved toward its escape.
But orders came to: "Keep the channel clear."
Nevada left the channel, went aground.

The last attack plane left Pearl Harbor at
about 9:50, making the attack
just short of two hours long. The focus turned
to tending to the wounded; fighting fires.

With carriers on missions out of port
and safe from the attack, the battleships
were prime objectives, but just two of eight
were lost; the rest, repaired, returned to sea.

Repair facilities were left unharmed;
an oversight for which Japan would pay.
A number of the ships they thought they sank
returned in force to fight another day.

The Navy lost more sailors than were killed
in all of World War I. The viciousness
led to a retribution that the world
had never seen, nor ever should again!

2.12 Overlord
D-Day, 6/6/44

In 1942, the Allied leadership concluded that eventually a head-on battle would be essential to defeat the Axis powers. After Germany invaded Russia, Stalin called on the Allies to attack Germany from the west to ease the pressure on Russian forces. Planning for opening a "western front" took over two years to bring to fruition; its code name was Operation Overlord.

Wind-driven rain pelted the makeshift headquarters
with such force, it made conversation difficult.
Present were senior military men, tasked with
conducting the largest invasion in history.

It was early morning 5 June 1944, the date selected
for the operation when May 1 was scrubbed
for shortage of landing craft. Heavy rain, high winds,
rough seas, and limited visibility cost the June 5 D-Day.

Discussions centered around reports of a short break
in the weather predicted for the following day.
Heavy surf conditions would continue, but
further delay involved problems of another sort.

A large fictitious army group in Southern England
had been created to serve as a deception. Information
had been leaked that this large force would attack
at Calais. Such large-scale secrets can only be kept so long.

Additionally, the phases of the moon and therefore
tides would soon be unfavorable for landing forces
on beaches. General Ike had these and other considerations
weighing on him; the final decision was his to make.

At 4:00am, June 5, General Eisenhower decided:
Operation Neptune, D-Day, would be June 6, 1944.
Thus began the Battle of Normandy,
one of the costliest victories in history.

Overlord involved 7,000 vessels from eight navies.
Of five adjacent landing beaches, U.S. forces
were assigned two: code named OMAHA and UTAH.
Neptune's greatest casualties would occur on OMAHA Beach.

Amphibious landings, faced with high surf, encountered
overturned and misdirected landing craft, seasick soldiers,
and intense enemy fire. Air and naval gunfire support
were limited because of low clouds and poor visibility.

Casualties were heavy, but wave after wave of soldiers
and equipment landed and advanced on enemy positions
behind the beaches. Limited enemy reinforcements suggested
that deception of the fake attack on Calais had worked.

Acts of bravery and sacrifice were commonplace
throughout that bloody day. Soldiers performed
heroic actions that were well beyond what they thought
were their limits. Sadly, many never left that beach.

Ensuing days saw intense fighting continuing,
as objectives of Overlord, driving enemy forces
from Western France, could not be achieved in a day.
On 30 August 1944, the enemy crossed the Seine in retreat.

The Battle of Normandy was finally over, marking
the beginning of the end of the war in Europe.
The cost to Allied Forces was over 200,000
casualties; nearly 50,000 died.

Those individual participants in this operation
found it impossible at the time to absorb the scope,
the magnitude of what they had been a part.
Their job - move on; prepare for the next battle.

Later, past their days of combat, they realized
they had played a role in a singular historic
event of monumental proportions. Survivors
still visit Normandy to honor friends that never left.

2.13 The Day of Glory
Easter Sunday

"It is finished!"
He had uttered just days ago -
but it wasn't.
His earthly mission - yes,
but not His legacy.

Did He cheat death?
Witnesses to the beating,
the scourging, the "crown," the death walk -
and finally the nails and the lance
know death was not cheated.
It was suffered in the most mortal way.
Evasion would hardly lead to glory.

The very human eleven were left in fear
to wonder what their future held.
But then, on that miracle morning,
a new history began.
By His return, His promises
and teaching were seen in light
with clarity that none had seen before.

Jesus had not cheated death;
He accepted it - then overcame it.
This Day of Glory showed the world
His relationship with God.
Millennia have passed since then,
and much forgotten,
but not His Words.

2.14 Labor Day

From dawn to dark you used God-given skills
to earn your daily bread.
With strength of arm and will of tempered steel,
you kept your fam'ly fed.

Our country's industry was built on you,
not those who started rich.
The annals of the working man found you
creating your own niche.

The lack of workers' voice left many needs
unmet and out of range.
But when you joined with others to rebel,
then things began to change.

From steel to coal to workers on the docks,
and many other trades,
your battles for your rights and better pay
were labor's own crusades.

Our forebears showed a strength of character
that paved for us the way.
Examining our past, with gratitude,
we honor you this day.

2.15 The Humble Queen
Mother's Day

Gusting winds sling sand that stings the skin,
this afternoon a kiln of arid air.
The man proceeds with measured pace ahead;
his youthful wife and burro close behind.

She plods on step by painful, grudging step;
her back aches, and her body yearns for rest.
But she could never yield to weakness now;
her mission clear - she has to carry on.

The barren land around belies her state;
maturing in her is the fruit of life.
This voyage forced upon them by decree;
she prays: *Protect my child till journey's end.*

Their balky beast of burden's jarring pace
evokes concern about untimely birth.
Her pact with God convinces her that she
must make this journey walking all the way.

When nighttime comes the winds turn cold as rime;
they badly need some shelter for their rest.
Ahead a light appears - it's Bethlehem,
the object of their trek at last in sight.

Without accommodations at the inn,
their journey ends within a stable stall.
Discomfort eases on the bed of straw;
her fear of the unknown denies her sleep.

Her visitation months before assured
that she'd conceive and bear the Son of God.
Her role beyond the birth a mystery;
she wonders what the future holds for her.

Before the night has ended pains begin;
unshakeable her faith and trust in God.
She lives to see the promised Son emerge
to make a temple of this lowly cave.

*   *   *   *   *   *   *

That God selected her to bear His Son
and raise Him in traditions of the day.
She then was witness to His painful death,
consoling Him until His final breath.

A score of centuries pass; we still revere
her courage and commitment to a dream.
At Christmas time we celebrate His birth,
and honor Mary, Mother for all time.

2.16 That Was My Dad
Father's Day

About six feet and large of girth,
he sold seeds, bulbs, and plants.
In high school he'd have done okay,
but never got the chance.
That was my dad.

Depression years and pay was low
the times for all were hard.
He took a risky part-time job:
a penitentiary guard.
That was my dad.

To earn some more he undertook
piano-moving work.
He had his children to support;
hard work he'd never shirk.
That *was* my dad.

Republican through to the core:
a self-reliant gent.
He had no use for whiners who
could never be content.
That was *my* dad.

That April day in forty-five
he called his boys inside.
He wanted us to witness news:
that final caisson ride.
That was my *dad*.

We "saw" them honor FDR
through radio's mystique.
With sadness I had never seen,
a tear ran down his cheek.
Was that my dad?

Dad drifted off in later years,
and alcohol took hold.
His mind went weak; his golden years
were anything but gold.
I *lost* my dad.

He died so many years ago
I hardly can recall.
We never spoke of love, I know;
We seldom spoke at all.
God bless my dad!

2.17 Cristoforo Colombo
Columbus Day

Born in Genoa in 1451,
Columbus, in his teens, went to sea.
Experienced at twenty-three, he sailed aboard a ship
to the isle of Khios in the Aegean.
Just two years later he was bound for England.
Off Cape St. Vincent, set upon by privateers,
Columbus' ship was burned and sank.
Clinging to floating wreckage,
he made his way to shore,
landing near Lagos. Soon he moved on to Lisbon
to continue his seaman's life in Portugal.

For years he sailed the seas as far as Iceland and Guinea,
but the dream to reach the riches of Marco Polo's Orient
by sailing west grew year by year.
When opportunity to propose his idea to King John
yielded nothing, Columbus moved to Spain.
King Ferdinand and Queen Isabella,
who yearned for trade with Asia,
accepted the Italian's plan, agreeing
to send three ships in search of routes to wealth.

On August 2, 1492, Columbus set sail from Spain
with *Niña*, *Pinta*, and flagship *Santa Maria*.
Educated people of the age accepted Earth as a globe,
but few conceived its size. He had no fear
of falling off the earth, but he can be forgiven
when, on October 12, 1492, he sighted the Bahamas, and
proclaimed that he had reached the East Indies.

What did this Italian adventurer, born Cristoforo Colombo,
sailing for Spain, really accomplish?
He was a European who faced the North Atlantic
in three small ships and discovered land
where Europeans had not been before -
and returned to tell his tale.

Excitement led to funding for explorers
who would follow in this burgeoning
age of exploration. Cabot, de Leon, Balboa,
Pizzaro, Magellan, Cortes, de Soto all played
their roles in bringing the Americas
into the civilized world.
This Genoa-born sailor led the way.

2.18 Gift of Gifts
Valentine Day Sonnet

You smile and sunshine shoos the clouds away,
you laugh: is that a lark's melodic song?
Your touch caresses like a breeze of May;
you're with me now and nothing will go wrong.

For many wondrous years we've shared our dreams,
some hopes fulfilled, and others left behind.
But those that lie ahead, or so it seems,
provide the spark to seek what we shall find.

The strife of life provides for all a test,
where some will fall, while others will survive,
and grow in love with feelings best expressed
in quiet times, where love is most alive.

Your smile, your laugh, your touch, your dreams, your love:
the gift of gifts to me from God above.

2.19 The Graduation Party
Graduation Day

Commencement is a joyful time,
a time to celebrate.
We took the long and tedious road,
and now we graduate.

Our friends and family cheer us on
with pride in what we've done.
Relief and hope and happiness
are all mixed into one.

We know that soon our lives will change,
but for tonight we raise
our glasses to the fun we had
throughout our student days.

As hours pass by and sound subsides
I sense a change in tone.
A sadness fills my classmates' eyes;
none want to be alone.

The truth of what is happening
begins to take effect.
The future starts; the past departs:
a time to just reflect

on days gone by and friends we've made,
some we'll not see again.
A melancholy mood prevails;
our joy is merged with pain.

Brave smiles are forced; farewells are said
to every long-held friend.
Commencement means "beginning," but
it also means an end.

2.20 Inauguration Day

The magic of democracy
presents itself this day.
Despite our many differences,
elections pave the way.
We show the world, with all our flaws,
real power on display.

Since we elect our president
just once in four long years,
the value of the vote we spent
must be on one who hears
the voices that election sent
to Washington with cheers.

Bullets, bombs, and tragic death
show weakness in resolve;
if one can't trust the ballot box,
the public to involve,
when problems are addressed with guns
solutions won't evolve.

We have our share of folks who would
obstruct the normal flow.
The system works with stunning ease
to stem the undertow.
Elections give us all a voice
in who directs our show.

This day when power changes hands,
regardless who has won,
the celebration unifies
with pride in what we've done.
We look ahead with joyful hope;
a new day has begun.

2.21 A Birthday Wish

Just once a year we owe ourselves
a day that brings us well-earned fun.
It may involve a group of friends
or just a very special one.

If music fills your heart with joy,
surround yourself with it this day.
If travel makes your life complete,
then plan a trip without delay.

If theater is your main love,
get tickets to a favorite play.
Or if the dance makes your heart race,
you will find beauty in ballet.

But only you can make the choice
since birthdays come just once a year.
Your friends sincerely wish for you
a day that's filled with love and cheer.

2.22 Octogenariosis
80th Birthday

Octogenariosis is
a disease I hope some day to catch.
I heard it attacked my friend Joseph;
the symptoms - an itch you can't scratch.

He thinks his good humor can hide it;
his attitude makes him seem young.
How come he won't act like the others:
you know, like a bow that's unstrung?

But no, he keeps acting so joyous;
his smile is both happy and sly.
I'd say he is putting us on,
for that twinkle is there in his eye!

So, octogenariosis,
you're welcome to take your best shot;
but focus on things that he can do,
don't waste time on what he cannot!

You must know, he's really not caught you,
although you infect many men.
For Joseph is not reaching eighty;
he's actually seventy-ten!

God bless!

Part 3: Events, Opinions, Tales

3.1 The New Dominion

Both nobly born and common man
from England crossed the sea,
and thus the Commonwealth began
with those who would be free

to spread themselves across the land
and settle where they could.
With hardships greater than they planned,
they still found freedom good.

From sturdy stock their leaders grew
with independent thought.
Protecting liberty, they knew,
could not be simply bought.

The price was high, but fully paid,
as brave men's blood was shed.
A nation then was loosely made;
Virginia's statesmen led.

The Commonwealth's diversity -
its greatest attribute,
with fishing from the bay and sea
and orchards filled with fruit.

The Shenandoah farms provide
fine food for rich and poor.
The massive rivers, long and wide,
link Blue Ridge to the shore.

The tempo of commercial north
contrasts with southern pace.
The eastern watermen go forth,
a wind-tossed sea to face.

A home for all who would be true
to those who paved the way,
the Old Dominion lives anew,
proud gem of USA.

3.2 On Being Non-White

Can we ignore what isn't right
when it's been wrong four hundred years?
To kill or maim to show our might,
survivors left to drown in tears?

How could forebears not realize
how inhumane it was to see
the evil dance before their eyes
yet take no steps to disagree?

> They understand that they are free,
> but seldom find equality.

The opportunities for whites
in education, jobs, and health
are often called their human rights
that open doors to gaining wealth.

For non-whites things are not the same,
they often hear 'that same old song'
with attitudes that should hold shame
but just imply: "You don't belong."

> They understand that they are free,
> but seldom find equality.

In uniform they fought with pride,
but now a uniform means fear.
Police will pull non-whites aside
as if non-whites pose threats severe.

For many, faith renews their strength,
and hope says wrongs may soon be right.
For love they'll go to any length
in prayer to make their future bright.

> They understand that they are free,
> but seldom find equality.

3.3 Life's Referee *(An English Sonnet)*

The umpire makes those crucial judgment calls,
including if a runner's safe or out.
He also rates the pitches strikes or balls.
Decision-making is what he's about.

A football referee has complex rules;
a judgment call can often cause dispute.
Now instant replay is among his tools,
but patience is his greatest attribute.

For those of us engaged in life's great game
whose job is it to guarantee fair play?
Our parents, teachers, clergy take the blame
when someone's moral values go astray.

But in a free society free will
is not a license to ignore the laws
or step upon the rights of others, till
you cross a fateful line another draws.

Fair play is our responsibility;
we must become our moral referee.

3.4 '55 at Fifty

(A tribute to the USNA Class of 1955 on its 50th reunion)

From all across the forty-eight, we came
and gathered in July of fifty-one.
Harry Truman was our leader's name;
Korea's war was far from being done.

For four long years we struggled to become
the type of leaders people would respect.
On Graduation Day we would succumb
to heady dreams of lives we might expect.

We soon learned leaders need to be inspired
before they're proven worthy of their stripes.
We imitated those whom we admired,
but found we really had no prototypes.

As individuals we made our way
through complex mazes each of us would face.
As time went on, some heard the call to say
"farewell" - and other ventures they'd embrace.

Regardless of the field, there was success,
and heartbreak every time we took a loss.
Our fallen classmates forced us to address
the omnipresence of the albatross.

Now fifty years since when we tossed our caps,
embarking on a life we barely knew,
we still get misty-eyed when we hear "Taps",
and "Blue and Gold" excites our hearts anew.

We sailed the seven seas and flew the skies,
and fought our country's battles on the ground.
Our classmates passed life's tests with steady eyes;
adventures that we sought we surely found.

When age and wisdom seem to coincide,
we realize our work was not in vain.
Whatever role we played, we could take pride;
we'd been a link in that unbroken chain.

3.5 The Gale

Scarlet sky at sunup
forewarns the seasoned observer.
Majestic, towering clouds, silver-lined, growing.
Sun dissolves into troubled heavens.
Rain starts downward, then sideways,
bullied by lashing, random gusts.

A battle rages here.
Somber hues foretell the risk to interlopers
who might dare to venture onto this battlefield.
A private fight!
Superior strength of the sky
challenging the sovereign supremacy of the sea.

Birds have known the fury of this strife before,
their flight confused, fear fills their eyes.
They want to flee.
There will be no escape for them today
for they are chosen witnesses
to see the conflict to its end.

Angry clouds reach down to smite the waves
and demand surrender.
The sea responds with roiling hills,
their silver wind-blown manes
reflecting their disdain;
the struggle continues into night.
Darkness makes the war grow more intense;
both sides put inexhaustible power on display.
Massive sea swells heave ever upward.
The sky replies with brilliant streaks,
and roaring rumbling blasts.
Thunderbolts intimidate all
except the sea.

****

The next day dawns:
some drifting clouds still dripping night,
blow by, exposing
a sparkling, sun-filled sky,
the sea a peaceful pool.
How did the conflict end?
Only the winged observers know,
and they can never tell.

3.6 The Would-Be Poet

I didn't spend a lifetime writing rhymes,
I spent it living.
So why start now in these retirement times,
a sense of giving?
No, not at all. I just have lots to say,
and not much time.
So poetry may let me have my day
in bliss sublime.

And so I took my pen in hand because
I thought I could.
I wrote a verse, then checked it out for flaws.
Oh my, it's good.
I liked it, so I tried my skill once more.
Results? The same.
Another masterpiece that I thought bore
the mark of fame.

The time had come to share my work with Kate,
my learned friend.
She read the work that I had done to date
from end to end.
She said, "I think your talent's mediocre."
That's what she said!
I fought the urge to just get up and poke her,
but left instead.

So why spend precious time creating things
that folks berate?
Because, of course, to me the joy it brings.
I think they're great.

You think that I exaggerate???
That Kate was right on track??
Oh no, I know my talent's great!
It's ego that I lack!!

3.7 Oxymoron

Oxymoron is the neatest word;
it slides across my tongue like warm ice cream.
I use it every time I get the chance;
so for this poem, it will be the theme.

It means a combination of two words
that bicker like two siblings often do:
like joyful sadness, fascinating bore,
a brilliant dolt, or ancient ingenue.

If you are ill and your good doctor says:
"I think your problem is acutely chronic."
He's open for the following retort:
"But Doctor, isn't that oxymoronic?"

3.8 The Leader is ...

the one they look to when they've lost their way;
the one who raises spirits when they're down;
the one who will go back to help a stray;
the one who leads, but never wears a crown;

the one who will endure the daily pain;
the one who will provide the needed spark;
the one who works for good, not just for gain;
the one who finds the light amid the dark;

the one who stands apart, though in a crowd;
the one who will solve problems that arise;
the one who always speaks the truth aloud;
the one who will support, not criticize;

the one who listens to another's view;
the one who lives with energy and verve;
the one who will commit and follow through.
The leader is the one who's called to serve.

3.9 Katrina's Legacy
(August 2005)

Her glancing blow that stole
the sunshine from the Sunshine State
left us with almost casual thought:
another nasty storm.
But in the days ahead she became full-grown,
salivating over her next victim;
she took her time to savor what would come.
Dreaming of her name in history books,
she attacked the most defenseless prey.

Warnings in New Orleans went unheeded:
"After all we handled *Camille*, didn't we?"
Too late they learned this was much more.
The poor, when told to go, did not know where,
or if they did, lacked the means to get there.
Lashing winds made buildings dance
before collapsing into matchsticks.
The Gulf engulfed all that dared to dare.
Land, life and livelihood succumbed.

Before departing, she fired
one more lethal shot
to elevate herself from common killer
to epic mass murderer.
As dikes were breached
when she moved north,
water flooded south.
The sight of death afloat is etched
forever in our minds.
We have no power to evacuate
images of dismal decomposing death:
1,833 fatalities,
Katrina's legacy.

3.10 The Power of Evil
(A Sestina)

In Littleton, a sun-filled day in spring,
the pale green world emerges from the cold.
Crocus blossoms strain to find the light,
and mountain bluebirds seek their nests in pairs.
Columbine adds beauty to the scene;
the season sings of celebrating life.

As morning grows, the schoolyard comes to life
with joyful sounds as children nimbly spring
from sleepy buses to this busy scene.
Forgotten now is winter's bitter cold
as students stroll along the walks in pairs
then disappear where shadows hide the light.

Classes start; a normal day with sunlight
streaming through the windows. Inside, life
goes on, no unexpected noise impairs
the day's routine. No hint of what would spring
from tortured minds to catch these children cold
and turn this peaceful day to bloody scene.

Exploding guns transform the study scene
into chaotic fright. The former light
mood of the day transforms to deadly cold
as children scream and bodies fall, the life
blood leaking, pooling like a crimson spring:
demonic acts performed by Satan's pair.

Those parents viewing tragedy despair;
their child has not emerged from jumbled scene.
The television's eye seems poised to spring
on them the news all parents dread. The light
of hope begins to wane as loss of life
reports sustained by bodies stiff and cold.

The killers of these youth seem distant, cold;
their courage bolstered, working as a pair.
Commitment to a code, each took his life
to punctuate the senseless, tragic scene,
denying all survivors further light
about this devastating day of spring.

Next day, spring once again brings somber cold;
as light snow falls, the mourners walk in pairs,
this ghastly scene to view and hold for life.

3.11 Mercury

...achieving the goal, before this decade is out,
of landing a man on the moon and returning him
safely to the earth. ... J.F. Kennedy, May 25, 1961

While cameras clicked to capture Alan's smile,
he crawled into his saucer-shaped cocoon.
His mission was the perilous first step
that could someday land man upon the moon.

No matter what the outcome, it was clear:
succeed or fail, the journey wouldn't last.
The gentle landing in the Navy's realm
provided sharp contrast to lift-off's blast.

When Gus shot off, the confidence was high;
but still, the awesome lift-off gave us pause.
As parachute deployed we breathed a sigh,
another mission ending without flaws.

However, bobbing in the waves disturbed
the spaceman's stomach and he felt quite ill.
He was extracted but his coffin sank;
this day would not his destiny fulfill.

The final, longer flight belonged to John;
his mission - gird the globe, then back to Earth.
The images displayed enthralled us all;
successes of the program proved its worth.

As later tragedies would demonstrate
the risks that such a daring program brings.
We must salute these brave men who allowed
the goal that JFK proclaimed take wings.

3.12 The Lighthouse Keeper

The lighthouse keeper leads a lonely life;
for days on end he sees no living thing.
His world much smaller since he lost his wife,
and winter's cold brings prayers for early spring.

He well knows the importance of his light,
especially in storms when waves are high
and visibility is poor at night.
His beacon's always there; ships can rely.

His monthly trips to town to buy supplies
are welcome breaks from normal day's routine.
He learns of local issues that arise,
and he and Walt discuss the federal scene.

Walt runs the country store himself; he lost
his faithful wife who worked the store with him.
Two widowers decried the rising cost
of food, and means of cutting spending slim.

But as the afternoon wore on, he knew
his sense of duty called him home by dark.
There was no one to say "you're overdue,"
but loyalty to his light left its mark.

"Now you take care," Walt calls when he departs.
"You do the same," he answers his old friend.
Approaching home brings joy his light imparts;
his love for it he cannot comprehend.

3.13 My Love
An English Sonnet

I've never met one like her, that I know;
her pure commitment to me makes me strong.
My work keeps me quite busy now, although
she wiles away the hours all day long.

Her looks are not exceptional, I guess,
but beauty wasn't what I sought from her.
Companionship without a lot of stress -
and not excessive talking - I prefer.

She's getting rather paunchy, I admit,
but she finds exercise no longer fun.
At dinner time I hardly get to sit
before I note that she's completely done.

But looks and manners never will prevail;
I know I'm loved - the way she wags her tail.

3.14 Legacy

We never know what legacy
was ours from day of birth.
And yet we strive from day to day
throughout our time on Earth.

Accomplishments just come and go
but we cannot assess
if what we did and left behind
brings joy and happiness

to those who meant the most to us
when life was ours to spend;
and did we treat each one we met
like we would treat a friend?

Might there be things that we regret
and wish we hadn't done?
Commit today to make things right;
make peace with everyone.

Our lives have purpose; that we know.
But where we fit, we learn
from what we do; how hard we work
and whose respect we earn.

If you would write your own obit
that shows you at your best,
is that the you, you are today?
If so, you pass the test.

Otherwise.....

3.15 How Are You?
(On meeting an old friend on the street)

"How are you?" I ask, as if I'm not aware,
but it seems like the right thing to say.
"I couldn't be better," he's quick to declare,
though he seems to be deep in decay.

"And how about you?" comes his requisite probe,
insincerity etched in his smile.
"I think I could whip any man on the globe,"
I retrieve from my large cliché file.

I truly feel awful and he looks the same,
so what makes us go through this routine?
Is there really shame if I loudly proclaim,
"I feel rotten and you look obscene?"

3.16 Evolution of Opinion

1960

My brother and I boarded the plane,
a business trip to San Diego
we had eagerly anticipated.
Our pilot welcomed us
with a smooth, standard spiel. I said,
"Do you see how old that geezer is?
I hope he doesn't have a heart attack
before we get to San Diego."
Yeah, I wonder when the airline
retires these guys. Did you notice
that woman that boarded ahead of us?
She must be 60, struggling to look 40.
"Why do they do that?"

2010

A long-awaited fishing adventure,
a Christmas present from our wives,
put Bob and me on a plane to Florida.
After a brief welcome by the pilot, I commented,
"I can't believe how these airlines
entrust the responsibility of the lives
of all these passengers to youngsters,
and is that co-pilot a girl?
Where's the experience?"
Yeah, I'd feel much more comfortable
if I saw two guys with some gray hair.
How about that woman across the aisle?
She must be about 60.
"Man, she's hot!"

3.17 The World To Be?

Strolling on this chill October morn,
cloudless sky; multi-hued leaves please my eyes
and elevate my spirits.

Schoolyard sounds attract me,
draw me to their source.
Spirited children scurry across the grounds.

Kick ball, dodge ball, hop scotch, tag;
white, black, brown, yellow;
everyone involved in this symphony of youth.

Cacophony becomes melody;
discord becomes harmony;
the beauty and simplicity of the scene stun me.

It looks so easy;
seems so natural;
what could turn this concert into dissonance?

They do not see differences;
they have a love of life;
their love is all-inclusive.

This is *not* the *world* that is;
might it be the world to be?
We pray.

3.18 The Journey Home

The paved road ended, turned to well-packed clay;
the cab climbed one last hill that led to home.
Bucolic beauty took my breath away;
I wondered why I ever chose to roam.

The mountain backdrop - how I missed this scene,
contrasting colors: shrubs and grass and trees.
I visualize a life here quite serene,
unlike my many years spent overseas.

The time had treated house and barn quite well;
my dad took pride in how his home appeared.
Perhaps his love of land made me rebel;
or maybe growing up like him, I feared.

Tomorrow when we lay my dad to rest,
an era ends - a manor less its lord.
Has owning this been my dream unprofessed?
Might he have left me this as my reward

for leaving home and never turning back?
He owed me nothing; that is understood.
His leadership kept my young life on track.
The accident changed both our lives for good.

Since I was driving, I took all the blame;
my carelessness had cost my mother's life.
From that day forward, things were not the same;
he shunned me as the one who killed his wife.

Was there forgiveness ever in his heart?
I doubt it - but I gave up long ago.
Had I returned, would he have played the part
of father in Luke's gospel? I don't know.

We near the house, my hands begin to shake;
recriminations flood into my head.
I know I caused my father's heart to break,
yet still, in death, to see him now I dread.

What will I find behind that large front door?
Will guilt remain with me forevermore?

3.19 The Time For Change

What makes a politician what he is?
When are his ideals suctioned from his head?
What makes him reach for things that just aren't his?
Who fills that trough to see that he is fed?

The Constitution says how they should play,
but lawmakers can bend the rules at will.
Their run for reelection starts the day
they take the oath; their futures to fulfill.

They also promise things they can't control,
and act like friends with people they can't stand.
Their speeches could replace my Demerol
with metaphors we all misunderstand.

Do you support incumbent's plaintive pleas
when he brings federal money to your zone?
Is that called statesmanship - or a disease
that we, the voters, openly condone?

They call it pork - but it's to buy your vote,
and Congress greets it with a wink and nod.
However, they condemn the budget's bloat,
"Let's cut the pork!" an often-heard façade.

Our legislators have become the slaves
of party, large contributors, and greed.
Decisions made in private, small conclaves
are seldom aimed at meeting nation's need.

Both parties' leaders - not by accident,
have yielded to the arrogance of power.
Their voting party lines - embarrassment:
but going against their party makes them cower!

Since soft campaign funds help them to succeed,
to pay off obligations is a must.
It seems that they no longer need to heed
that public service is a public trust.

I hardly think reform will be a goal
of those who sit in judgment on themselves.
A bill that might upset a leader's role
will find its final place on dusty shelves.

I know that we cannot begin anew
and form a system that would make more sense.
For instance, one where red states might turn blue,
and blue turn red based on the year's events.

Hello, you voters, when will you decide
that you, at last, have had enough of this?
The problems, we can see, are country-wide;
if we ignore them, are we not remiss?

Those there the longest should be first to go
so leadership can pass to newer hands.
Careers in Congress are not apropos;
complacency will not meet our demands.

Since we have means to make a peaceful change
what makes us sit and let this cancer grow?
It's frustrating, and yes it's even strange
that we would just accept the status quo.

So what will your response to these words be?
Perhaps a few of you may take a stand
and force your representative to see
your expectations and what you demand.

3.20 We The People

Our government is broken many ways
and fixing it will take some drastic change.
When wealth determines how our laws are made,
and ill-gained influence gets its reward,
while moral character can be ignored,
one hardly can expect one's voice be heard.

When party loyalty becomes the rule,
and disagreement looks like disrespect,
those "leaders" we elect just get in line
like lemmings blindly heading toward the cliff.

Of The People was the clear intent
of those brave men who gambled with their lives
to form a government that would be led
by those who best expressed the peoples' will
through fair elections. But the system's flaws
allowed a lesser candidate to thwart
the people's will; the system simply failed.

By The People once again told all
that those whom the electorate sends forth
to execute responsibilities,
the system should support and not abort.
A president appoints a judge to fill
a vacancy, that is his job to do.
One man, who's from a minor state, objects,
and on his own he stops the process cold.

For The People means that those in power
will live the doctors' oath: First do no harm.
But when the president and VP back
the Speaker's bill that would throw millions off
their health insurance plan, and implement
a tax cut for the rich, what would come next?

Assessing blame to individuals
does little to address the system's flaws.
We need to take a comprehensive look
at all the building blocks of governance.

Our citizens must have the will to change
if they expect their voices to be heard.
Our country's leadership is now on trial;
our children won't forgive if we allow
democracy to *perish from the earth*.

3.21 Green Mountain Magic

Our auto bumps along the gravel road;
a picnic on Mount Equinox we planned.
The engine whimpers at the climbing load,
but on we push till deep in timberland.

Continuing on foot we find a glade:
an overlook where we can see for miles.
The azure sky offsets the forest jade;
serenity of summertime beguiles.

A blanket spread for comfort, picnic starts,
we feel we are alone in Nature's world.
This setting is idyllic for sweethearts,
but caution flags refuse to be unfurled.

Enchantment of the moment overcomes
restraints and inhibitions of our youth.
The passion of the picnic soon succumbs
to promises encased in love and truth.

*   *   *   *   *   *   *

Some four decades have passed as now we drive
and mem'ry helps us find our parking spot.
The climb, a challenge now, but we arrive;
the clearing is still here, but changed somewhat.

A fuzzy haze diminishes our view;
the sky less blue, the pines and oaks less green.
But nonetheless our picnic would ensue;
though things had aged, this site remained serene.

Commitment to this day made years ago
drew us to Equinox this summer day.
Were hidden reasons there? We didn't know.
We spread the fruit and cheese and Chardonnay.

I look at her, my hands begin to shake;
I recognize we've entered love's domain.
At once the sleeping passions come awake;
our mountain works its magic once again.

3.22 Retirement Resolution

My days of working to survive
have passed me by, so what comes now?
Is this unending holiday?
Is this the rest life will allow?

Does my retirement stop my brain
or still my search for life's surprise?
I hardly think I can deny
my brain or body exercise.

God did not put me here to watch
and wait for strength and will to fade.
To put my skills to use each day
brings joy that I cannot evade.

So let these aging years pile up,
I'll not surrender to their threats.
As will and energy still live,
I'll journey on without regrets.

3.23 The Inglorious Face of War

His shuffling gait was punctuated by a pronounced limp;
a wide-brimmed hat of gray felt with large grease spots
shielded his eyes from the July sun.
He cradled a small brown bag of goods
against his red-checked flannel shirt,
buttoned at the neck, defying the tortuous heat.
His dark blue denim trousers with torn pockets
covered the tops of brown work boots,
heels well worn, soles wafer-thin.

"What's he doing in our neighborhood?
Stay on this side of the street, children!"
The thirtyish woman in the tailored jeans was annoyed.
"Shouldn't they put him away somewhere?"
The other woman asked rhetorically.
"What do we pay taxes for? Is there no protection
from having riff-raff like that in our town?"
His painful pace carried him clear of his critical observers,
of whom, he took no notice.

The unpainted, weathered door of his shack
creaked as he pushed it open, revealing one large room.
Kitchen was left rear; bedroom, right rear;
eating and living area, front.
He placed his precious groceries on the table,
alongside the yellowing picture
of an attractive dark-haired woman.
He stared at the picture, and memories stirred.
She'd been faithful and waited for him throughout the war,
then cared for him for years thereafter:
undying love, unbending spirit, unending commitment.

She nursed his body back to modest health.
He learned to walk, but pain was always there;
night terrors robbed his sleep of rest.
His working life had ended on that beach;
her part-time jobs filled just their basic needs.
One day, her gallant, loving heart beat its last.
Her loss, one final devastating blow:
no one to love; no one to care; no one to understand.
Days were long; nights interminable.

His meager pension kept him in this world,
a world he sorely wished to leave.

He eased onto the bed to sleep
and face his dream once more:
sand and rocks his bed at Anzio that fateful day.
Right leg shattered, bleeding, unable to move;

Morrison to his left, Bernstein to his right;
panic frozen on their faces.
They stare at him, eyes wide, seeing nothing.
"Someone help, ... please God, ... someone help ....."

3.24 Victory Garden
(as experienced by a 12-year old)

The concept that planting a vegetable garden
in rural upstate New York
could help win a war overseas
completely escaped me.
We weren't eliminating the enemy,
nor were we feeding our soldiers.
We planted, we weeded, we fertilized, we harvested;
then we ate like real farmers all winter.
Perhaps someday I'll understand this war thing.

Corn was easy to plant and tend.
I had studied how Indians planted corn in mounds;
five seed kernels and one dead fish per hill.
We planted in rows - and left out the fish.
When the corn grew, it had strong stalks,
green tasseled soldiers, never intimidated by weeds.
Corn-on-the-cob was the best (even with oleo).

I love carrots, especially raw,
crunchy, crisp, and sweet as jujubes,
but what a pain to grow.
The seeds are as small as pepper flakes,
and you plant them so shallow - you barely cover them.
They germinate far too close,
so they must be thinned - terribly tedious.
Weeds sprout up to dominate the tender plants,
but pulling a weed without uprooting several plants -
difficult! But what would a pot roast be without them?

My dad showed me how to cut seed potatoes
to ensure that each section contained a promising eye.
Potato hills were easy to keep tidy with a hoe,
and digging them up at the end was exciting;
you never knew how many you'd find in a hill.
Beets were like carrots, no fun - too much work.
When you pulled them up, they bled on your hands;
I didn't even like the taste of beets.

A damp spring produced a bountiful crop of peas;
I ate them raw out of the pods.
We really over-killed on string beans;
Mother canned about fifty quart Ball jars.

I guess I did enjoy the gardening experience
and it must have been successful:
you know, winning the war, and all.

3.25 The Killer Beast

My steps were halting on this somber night,
as autumn breezes made the dry leaves dance.
The drifting clouds consumed the harvest moon
and added darkness to my circumstance ...
Did I prepare?

I knew I shouldn't stray too far from home
since probably the killer's still around.
His mauling of my brother sickened all,
its impact on the neighborhood profound ...
A fear we share.

Bravado isn't normally my thing,
so caution, care, concern my credo here.
Was that a sound, a movement over there?
An acorn from an oak tree landed near ...
A silly scare!

Darkness can be friend or can be foe,
and sudden change can be inopportune.
Just thirty feet from safety and my home
the guardians of the dark disgorge the moon ...
And I just stare!!

My body froze, my heart was pounding now.
My breathing stopped, for there before my eyes
that terrifying sight - the killer thing,
a furry beast at least four times my size ...
His nostrils flare!

He hasn't seen me yet; I must not move;
to run would lead me to a nasty fate.
His focus elsewhere gives me time to think.
To breathe would be to hyperventilate ...
And I'll not dare!

Then suddenly he bounds off, not toward me;
instinctively I bolt from danger's way.
The beast was chasing yet another beast,
allowing me to see another day ...
Without despair!!
There is a moral to my tale, you see,
and it revolves around our habitats.
If you're a furry squirrel just like me,
select a neighborhood devoid of cats ...
Or else ... *beware!!!*

Part 4: Navy Experiences (Essays)

4.1 The Fish and Wildlife Officer

My initial assignment as a freshly-minted ensign, U.S. Navy, was assistant engineer officer aboard USS Colahan (DD-658) in San Diego. My first few months were spent becoming acclimated with the ship in general, the engineering plant in particular, learning the names and skills of my division's personnel, and adjusting to the life of a seagoing sailor. I knew that in a few months we would be deploying to the Western Pacific on a six-month cruise. Much preparation would be required before we took in all lines and headed toward the sunset. One part of that preparation came as a surprise just two weeks before departure.

Colahan was one of four ships in Destroyer Division 172, which, when coupled with the four destroyers of Division 171, formed Destroyer Squadron 17, the Seahorse Squadron. That label was attached when the squadron was formed shortly after World War II. I regale you with this trivia only because of its relevance to my story. At an officers' meeting in the wardroom two weeks before deployment, the captain announced that he wanted to have a fish tank installed in the wardroom and to inhabit the tank with a few seahorses; he obviously felt the squadron commander would be quite impressed with his creativity. That was the nature of my commanding officer. He thought that it should come under the purview of the engineering department, and said, "Lull, make it happen."

Although I had seen pictures of seahorses, I hadn't actually seen a real seahorse, let alone had any idea how or where they lived, what they ate, or how to treat them. What I did know for sure, after four years at the Naval Academy was how to respond to this weird bit of senior stupidity. Collecting all my creativity, I replied, "Aye, aye, sir."

My boss, the chief engineer, struggling to keep from breaking up, said: "Mr. Lull will assume the position of Fish and Wildlife Officer." While the other officers guffawed, I recalled a line that Zane Grey used in several of his westerns, "He smiled without mirth."

Had Wikipedia been available in those days, I'd have learned that the taxonomy of the genus hippocampus contains forty-seven varieties of these critters. Mercifully I did not have that information to further mess with my mind. The first task was to determine where in the wardroom a fish tank would fit and what logistics problems needed to be overcome to make an installation feasible that could safely remain in place on a rocking and rolling destroyer. Once the tank purchase and installation were underway, I needed to get to the main attraction - the seahorses. I did a quick study so I wouldn't look too dumb when I went to procure them.

Let me tell you a little about these creatures so this paper will have at least a minuscule amount of educational value. As shown in pictures, they swim upright by rapidly fluttering a dorsal fin, and steering with pectoral fins located behind their eyes. They are normally seen resting because they are poor swimmers. They have long snouts that they use to suck up food; their eyes operate independent of one another. Quite interesting - and very weird - is how they reproduce. When mating, the female deposits eggs in a brood pouch on the front side of the male seahorse. The male fertilizes the eggs and supplies them with prolactin. The brood pouch provides oxygen as well as an incubator environment for the eggs to hatch within the pouch after a gestation period of two to four weeks. When the very fat male finally expels 100-200 fully developed seahorses, the parents have little to do with the offspring; they are good to go. Now here is the tough part. The male typically gives birth at night, and by morning is ready for the next batch of eggs. This guy is a sex machine, as is his funny-looking babe. I could go further into the gestation routines, but this is a PG-13 story.

When I located a pet store that had a wide variety of fish for sale, I asked a sales clerk about little seahorses; she said they stocked the dwarf variety of seahorses. I described what I was looking for and gave her the size of the tank we were installing. The woman seemed to be quite knowledgeable about these little fish; she assured me that the tank was large enough to house a few seahorses. She also informed me of the temperature ranges necessary and the importance of keeping a bubbling air supply in the tank. I asked her what they ate, and she replied, "Brine shrimp." When I told her we would be away from San Diego for a long time and asked where I would get brine shrimp to feed the fish. She pulled a box off a shelf and told me this supply of brine shrimp eggs would hold me for a year. "Just drop some eggs in water and they will hatch. Then you scoop the live shrimp out and drop them into the tank."

"One moment," I said, "What am I scooping the live shrimp from?"

"The brine shrimp tank," she said.

"I don't have a brine shrimp tank. Can't I just drop the eggs in the seahorse tank?"

"No," she said firmly. "If a seahorse ingests part of an egg shell, it would be fatal."

"What do I scoop the shrimp with," I asked. Off another shelf, she produced a mini-net.

"Make sure," she added, "that you start with fresh sea water in the tank." I left the store and hustled back to the ship to tackle the brine shrimp tank problem; fortunately, my boss agreed to take that off my plate.

The following day my wife and I went to the ocean side of Coronado with buckets to collect fresh sea water. *Colahan* was moored in the harbor at 32nd Street, hardly a source of fresh sea water. While milling around on some rocks, in my khaki uniform, bucket in hand, trying to not slip off into the water, a Navy helicopter came buzzing by. Although the pilot hovered overhead, probably wondering what I was doing, I went about my business. I really did not want to have to explain what I was doing out there to any sane person. Evelyn and I collected the water I needed as quickly as possible, loaded the full buckets into the car, and left. She said as I dropped her off, "this supply won't last long; where will you get fresh sea water next week?" I looked at her; she looked at me. Finally she said, "Oh, that's right; you'll be floating on it."

Returning to the ship, I brought the water aboard, set up the tank, tested it, checked out the newly installed brine shrimp tank, and decided I was ready to get the seahorses. I went to the store, bought the net, eggs, and the precious, little long-nosed fish. Back aboard, I ceremoniously deposited the seahorses into their new home and dropped a few eggs into the brine shrimp tank. That evening I was like a nervous new dad, wondering if my offspring would survive the night.

When I arrived the next day, the duty officer informed me that the funny-looking recruits I had shanghaied were still swimming. I was relieved, and collected my receipts to get reimbursement from the supply officer. He reviewed them and handed them back to me, saying, "When the squadron supply officer audits me, he'd love to gig me for spending taxpayers' money frivolously just so you can get in good with the captain." He was two grades senior to me and didn't like me much. He added, "Go see the welfare and recreation officer; see if he feels those funds can be used for crap like this." That last part especially irritated me on two counts. First, he knew welfare and rec funds were not to be spent for anything that didn't benefit the crew - these seahorses didn't benefit anyone. Second, he also knew that I was the welfare and recreation officer. I went to my desk, fingering the receipts I had been stiffed for, and thought - maybe I'm not cut out to be a seagoing sailor.

Two weeks later, we arrived at Pearl Harbor and moored. We would take on fresh supplies and fix any problems that had arisen on the first leg of the trip to WestPac. Also, we knew the squadron commander would come aboard to speak with the captain and see how the ship had fared the crossing. The captain was almost giddy about having this opportunity to show off his Seahorse Squadron mascots. The officers were assembled in the wardroom when the captain entered and proudly displayed his pets. The commodore's reaction was classic - he just stared into the tank, no smile, just a perfectly blank look. The captain broke the silence, "Ensign Lull has been in charge of the seahorses."

The commodore looked at me with what appeared to be an expression of sympathy in his eyes. He said, "Keep up the good work, Ensign." I was on deck when the commodore left. As he reached the dry-land end of the brow, his head was shaking from side to side. If I could put words to his thoughts they would be, *Seahorses? Seahorses? What idiot at the bureau sent me this clown to command a man of war?* Well, those probably weren't his thoughts, but they were mine.

After a few days' rest, we headed out for the next leg of our journey, during which we conducted a number of training exercises before stopping off at Midway Island to refuel. The next day we were underway again, en route to our first WestPac port of call, Yokosuka, Japan. By this time I had made friends with my charges and hadn't lost a single one. The captain was happy about that so, let us say, life was good. We were moored alongside a destroyer tender to get some maintenance and repair work done while in port. Only two of the squadron ships were in Yokosuka at the time, and our next leg would be a solo voyage to Subic Bay in the Philippines. Before getting underway, we had received the information that a tropical storm was brewing around Marshall Islands and heading slowly west. It wasn't a problem, but bore watching. When we went out, we headed dead east for a while, then began the journey south. The weather reports indicated that the storm was building and, at that time, appeared to be headed toward the Philippine Sea, perhaps to touch land at Luzon. In two days, the low had deepened, the wind strength grew, and the direction had turned northwest. It was now typhoon strength heading toward Taiwan, indicating we should pass well east of the anticipated track. We changed our course to southwesterly toward the Philippines to pass behind this nasty storm.

The following day, we received a disturbing report; the typhoon had made a surprising turn to the northeast. Taiwan dodged a bullet; we didn't. Storm reporting in those days did not have the precision that we have today, and the computer models used for projecting tracks did not exist. It is not an exacting science even with the models, but in the 1950s, data available was significantly less than today, and data processing was rudimentary. In this case, Taiwan, mainland China, and Japan would be spared a scary experience; *USS Colahan* would not. We were not only in the path of a typhoon, we would be in the dangerous semicircle. In olden days, the cry onboard would be, "Batten down the hatches!" All departments spent the day scouring their compartments to secure anything that could become a missile hazard in the height of the storm. A storm that size could do considerable damage even to a ship longer than a football field - like a destroyer - and in World War II even capsized some.

As a midshipman on cruise, I had experienced a hurricane at sea - but that was aboard an aircraft carrier. With its rather broad, high bow, broad beam, and deep draft, it rode differently from a sleek destroyer. It was a very bumpy ride. We rolled over forty degrees when caught in the trough and were pounded on the bow and superstructure when heading into the sea. In a high sea where waves and swell are thirty to forty feet, it's quite dangerous to run before the sea, that is, put the sea astern. At times, like slow motion, a large wave lifts the stern, holding the bow down and rendering the rudder useless. The ship goes where the sea dictates, not where the conning officer wants it to go. To make matters worse, the wind from astern carries the stack gases forward, choking the men on the bridge who are trying to control the ship. Cooking is impossible, so cold rations are passed around occasionally. Needless to say, the heads are constantly busy ... and messy. At night, all the problems of the day were magnified. When the ship began riding differently, we used spotlights to see if the sea had changed directions. Fortunately, we started from Yokosuka with a full load of fuel. Running out of fuel in a storm would be a disaster. Also, as fuel tanks emptied, we flooded them with sea water to keep from riding too high in the water and losing stability.

On the whole, we emerged from the experience relatively unscathed; lots of bumps and bruises from being tossed around, and some steel railings were twisted and would need to be replaced. However, when I went to the wardroom, I found that the two fish tanks had withstood the violent pounding that the ship had taken, but the inhabitants hadn't. The seahorses were on the surface, belly up. When I informed the captain, he said, "Okay, get rid of them and clean out the tanks." I did not conduct a burial-at-sea ceremony; in fact, I just flushed them down the toilet. I guess a typhoon experience reduces one's sensitivity.

4.2 ".... Just Keep That Equation Balanced."

In 1957, as a young naval officer aboard a destroyer, I decided that I would like to apply for submarine school and change my career path to undersea warfare. The mystique of the submarine service fascinated me, and the possibility of becoming part of a tight-knit, small, elite force was enticing. My commanding officer thought I was crazy, but I persisted. He forwarded my application and, to my surprise, I was selected. Having passed the first hurdle, I wondered if I would overcome the many stumbling blocks that contributed to the culling process that was part of the six-month course. Our first class lecture, given by the commander of the school, included the following general advice, "The secret to successful submarining is this: the number of dives must equal the number of surfacings. Just keep that equation balanced."

At the time I entered sub school, there were 120 submarines in the force, two of them nuclear: *Nautilus* and *Sea Wolf.* The studies were difficult for me because much of what I had learned from three years in a destroyer was irrelevant. Operational concepts, engineering considerations, buoyancy concerns, communication limitations, weaponry, attack tactics and just operating in three dimensions were all new and complex. Additionally, wherever I went on the submarine base, New London, I could see that 110-foot water tower, where escape training would be conducted, hovering menacingly over everything.

So, this story is about submarining, especially diesel-electric submarining. Most people know little about these ships, other than they have historically been called boats even though they really are ships. Submariners have been called the silent service. Why? During World War II, an intelligence briefing to congress revealed the operating and test depths of U.S. submarines. Despite the classification of that briefing, a loose-lipped congressman revealed the information in an interview. Up to that time, the Japanese had undercalled those depths by 100 feet, a fact that enabled many submarines to survive depth charge attacks. Depth charges are set to explode at preset depths. The cost of that slip is undetermined, but the effect was to seal lips. Even submarine losses were not well known. Our Navy lost fifty-two submarines in WW II, most in the Pacific and most with all hands, those we refer to as "shipmates still on patrol."

Although that information on diesel-electric subs is as irrelevant as diesel-electric subs in a nuclear submarine Navy, I thought you might find some things about this piece of history interesting. First, the evolution of submarines might be categorized into three phases. From the earliest subs through WW II, submarines were surface ships that could operate submerged for limited periods. The advent of German technology called the snorkel (after WW II) created a ship that could operate equally well surfaced or submerged. The third phase, nuclear power, brought the Navy a true submersible, a ship designed to operate continuously submerged. My experience, and this story, is about Phase 2, the force that was the mainstay of the submarine Navy during most of the Cold War.

You may notice that I am careful to refer to subs as diesel-electric, not just diesel. This is to differentiate from earlier submarines that were propelled by diesel engines, connected through gears to the propeller shafts. Diesel-electric boats had either three or four diesel engines (depending on the class) made by Fairbanks-Morse or General Motors, with attached generators. These powerful engineering combinations produced electricity to run the motors that drove the ships, charge the batteries, or both. For someone accustomed to relatively small electrical units, the power generated by these engine-generator combinations was prodigious. For example, when a battery charge was initiated while the submarine was at sea, the generators produced 3,000 amps at 250 volts for the charge while running the propulsion motors and auxiliary equipment. Depending on the class, each submarine had two or four batteries. Each battery had 126 cells; each cell produced two volts but weighed a ton. To get maximum speed, batteries were connected in series, producing 500 volts.

Well, enough about engineering. Very few diesel-electric subs were built after the war. Most of the force consisted of hulls built during the war and converted after the war to add the snorkel capability, get rid of deck guns (that had limited reliability), and update operational and weaponry equipment. I served in four such subs, two in the Pacific and two in the Atlantic. These were Guppy-class subs with superstructure and sail painted black. Periscopes and retractable masts protruded from the top of the sail; the length - any guesses? Much to the surprise of most, these little boats extended slightly longer than a football field. They were longer than many of the nuclear attack boats that followed.

Back to sub school, successful completion of escape training was a requirement for graduation. The training was designed to teach students how to escape from a sunken submarine that had no way of surfacing and no other form of rescue could be anticipated. The other unspoken purpose was to uncover latent claustrophobia. The first phase was classroom explanation of the tank and escape chamber layout, then a detailed description of the process of escape. On the designated day, about eight students plus an instructor were lowered thirty-five feet by elevator from the top of the tank to the chamber and herded inside each wearing swim trunks and an inflatable life preserver. The clearance from my head to the pipes that lined the overhead was but a few inches. We stood body-to-body awaiting the inevitable. The instructor, stationed next to the water-tight door that was the entrance to the tank, thirty-five feet below the surface, casually undogged the door. We had to trust that whatever law of physics said that the pressure outside that circular door would keep it shut would not be repealed that day. He then turned a valve that began flooding the chamber, while a vent at the top was open, keeping us at atmospheric pressure until the water was over the top of the combing - shoulder deep for me, chin deep for some. By this time, if a panic attack were to occur, it probably would have happened. The instructor then shut the vent, and cracked another valve to admit compressed air. We breathed normally and tried to clear our ears as the pressure built. When the pressure in the chamber reached the pressure in the tank, the circular door swung open. The instructor touched my shoulder to signal it was my time to go. I took three deep breaths, held the last, and squatted to go under the surface. With my left hand I reached through the door, grasping the upper combing. I put my left leg through the door, sat on the lower combing, then swung my right leg through. I was now completely in the tank, holding the upper combing. Next I pulled the cord to inflate the preserver, put my chin up, blew the air out of my lungs, let go and began my buoyant ascent. What seemed like minutes was really seconds until I broke the surface. Out of the water there were comments like: "No sweat" or "Piece of cake" even "That was fun!" However, the nervous laughter said volumes about our knowledge of how quickly an air embolism can be lethal, but we had made it!

Let's talk about buoyancy for a minute. A surface ship, including a submarine on the surface, displaces its own weight of water. A submerged object displaces its own volume of water. Ideally a submarine operating submerged is neutrally buoyant. That is, the water it displaces is equal to its weight and volume. The submarine is basically double hulled. The inner hull is the pressure hull, designed to withstand pressures up to the sub's test depth. The outer hull is made of much lighter gauge steel. The space between the two hulls serves as ballast tanks and fuel tanks. These tanks are constantly open to sea pressure, even the fuel tanks; therefore with sea pressure inside and outside the outer skin, it needn't be strong. The inner hull, however, has sea pressure outside and atmospheric pressure inside so it must be strong. Its strength comes from the thickness of the steel and its circularity. A cross section of the hull would reveal a circle - the ideal shape to withstand external pressures. The ballast tanks, called saddle tanks around the hull, are open to the sea underneath, whether on the surface or submerged. On the surface, however, the vents atop the tanks are shut. To submerge, the vents are opened and the tanks fill rapidly. As the sub goes down, the bow and stern planes are manned to take the ship to the depth designated and fly it through the water in level flight. As the submarine slows and the planes have less effect, we find how close to neutral buoyancy the sub is. Obviously, if the sub wants to rise, it's light; if it tends downward, it's heavy. To accommodate that, one can flood water in or pump water out of any of four tanks: one forward, one aft, two amidships, port and starboard. The operation is called trimming; the tanks are trim tanks. As the submarine operates submerged, its weight changes as stores are consumed, garbage is flushed, and, if snorkeling, fuel is used. The diving officer must be tuned in to these things, and trim the ship, as needed.

The submarine's primary sensor was state-of-the-art passive sonar. Historically, in submarine parlance, there were only two classes of ships: submarines and targets. That changed as I'll explain in a few minutes. With passive sonar, the skilled sonarman could detect, analyze, classify, and track sound sources that were many, many miles away. He also could be deafened by a pod of whales, a school of dolphins, or a bed of snapping shrimp. If he detected a ship, he could normally identify the class of ship, like light combatant, heavy combatant, merchantman, snorkeling sub, etc. simply by the quality of the sound. He could get an accurate bearing, a bearing rate and a turn count on the screws, but could only get a broad estimate on the range. Range information could be obtained by using the active sonar, but submarines only put sound energy in the water in an emergency. Stealth is a great advantage for subs; active sonar compromises stealth. Plotting techniques are normally relied upon for range estimates. Radar is available, but is seldom used during a classified mission. Course, speed, range and bearing are inputs to solve the fire control problem for a torpedo attack.

Electronic countermeasures are valuable sensor systems. Electronic emissions from other sources can be received, recorded, and analyzed to provide a wealth of information about the goings-on in the area in which you are operating. Radio equipment allows for communication on UHF, VHF, and HF frequencies, and receive-only on VLF for world-wide broadcasts.

During WW II, the primary mission for submarines was clear: interdict and sink enemy vessels. During the Cold War, that primary mission changed. Although submarines were used extensively during those years for intelligence gathering, the primary mission, the one that most training was devoted to, was anti-submarine warfare: locating, attacking, and sinking enemy submarines. That was the most exciting and nerve-wracking evolution of all. Two subs in near proximity with only passive sonar as a useful sensor is a very eerie operation. Fortunately, during the Cold War, to the best of my knowledge, no subs actually launched a live attack against another. Of course, we were not really at war, were we? But when gathering intelligence in waters our adversary claimed as his own, we had to be prepared for anything if detected. There was no back-up; we were absolutely on our own. We were not allowed to communicate, nor transmit any active signals, radio waves or sound. Navigation was dicey at best. Even our force commander didn't know where we were at any time during the two-month patrol; he only knew that we were in the large, predefined area to which we had been assigned. We had no doctor and no chaplain. Every bunk was occupied by someone contributing to the success of the mission. Not to be too dramatic, but if on the first day of our patrol, we suffered a flooding casualty that took us to the bottom, we would not be missed for over two months. In fact, the submarine would probably never be found. I shall never forget those patrols.

The weaponry in these subs included a left-over from WW II, the Mark 14 torpedo. It was twenty-one inches in diameter and about twenty feet in length, and traveled at forty-five knots, a very powerful weapon against surface targets. It was propelled by a steam system that burned alcohol, supported by compressed air. The steam ran turbines connected to the propellers. The problem: the products of combustion were soluble in water except for the nitrogen; hence the big nasty fish left a wake. A follow-on, the Mk 16, used hydrogen peroxide to provide oxygen to support combustion. The wake was gone, but we were left with the hazards of handling concentrated H_2O_2 in a closed environment. After the submarine mission changed, these torpedoes remained, because attacking surface targets would always be a secondary mission. However, the need for homing weapons to take on other subs was met with the Mk-37 torpedo. It contained passive and active sonars and was powered by a battery and motor. It was slow, but could be fired at a target when accurate range information was not available. It could be fired on a bearing that led the target on a snake course with passive sonar activated. When it detected the target, it would shift to a straight course, homing on the noise source. When the signal strength reached a preset level, the sonar shifted to active mode, homing on the actual target, foiling any noise makers that may have put in the water. Later a wire-guided version of this torpedo enabled the firing submarine to "drive" the weapon toward the noise source to the point that the weapon acquired the target and began homing on its own.

Well, enough of this technical stuff, let me relate my most enjoyable event in my submarine career. I went into the Navy with a strong wish to travel - and travel I did. When stationed in San Diego, I visited Alaska and Hawaii before they were states, several cities in Japan, Hong Kong, the Philippines, Bangkok and others. When on the East Coast I got to various ports in the Caribbean, Nova Scotia, England several times, Gibraltar, southern and northern Italy, southern France, southern Spain, Crete, Malta, and Majorca. But the best of all was when I was executive officer of *USS Halfbeak* and we visited Monte Carlo for Christmas 1965. When we arrived, there were invitations awaiting us for three officers to attend Midnight Mass and supper afterward with the royal family. The three senior officers, the skipper, Art Moreau, Rod Friedmann, and I volunteered for this tedious assignment. A limo picked us up at the appointed time and took us to the palace. Mass was held in the royal chapel in the palace; it was low-key, sedate, and reverent. Afterward, we were shown into the dining room that had a beautifully-set table and a large Christmas tree in a corner. The royal couple introduced themselves to us individually; then we sat for supper. Following supper, we gathered around the tree for light conversation, and Princess Grace presented each of us with a small Christmas gift. Good-byes were said and we were spirited back to our "luxurious" quarters aboard *Halfbeak*. As you can see, it was an experience I am not likely to forget. Perhaps the most disarming thing about the evening was not Princess Grace's beauty; we all knew about that long before the visit. It was the warmth and friendliness shown us by Prince Ranier. He was indeed the most gracious of hosts. If you wonder about the gift, it was a tie from Simpson of Piccadilly. It's my Princess Grace tie.

My years in submarines had some good times, some hard times, some real excitement, and some very boring times. But I am able to share this with you because - well - my shipmates and I kept that all-important equation balanced.

4.3 Surf's Up

It was a beautiful spring morning in Coronado as I left home at 6am to head for my ship berthed at the Naval Station, 32nd Street - the south side of San Diego. The date was Monday, May 23, 1960. I had my radio on as I made my left turn onto Orange Avenue and headed toward the ferry. The news was dominated by sporadic reports of a significant earthquake in Chile. When I took my place in the ferry line, I noticed it was somewhat longer than usual. I was scheduled as OOD that day to get *USS Razorback* underway, and drive it through the lengthy San Diego Harbor channel and out to sea; I could not afford to be late. When the ferry showed up, it was coming from a strange direction. It made an ugly smash landing in the slip, and the pilot stomped off the boat, cursing with every step. He was scared, and it became clear that things were not normal in the harbor. A more experienced pilot said he would make a run with the newest and most powerful ferry. My car was one of the last to board. We made it across safely and I headed for the base. I learned subsequently that the ferry service stopped for three hours after the one I had ridden made it across. The radio was now using that Japanese word we didn't hear too often: tsunami. Having taken a brief course at Scripps Institute of Oceanography, I knew what it was and what it wasn't.

At 0800, I backed the submarine from its berth, then turned it northward into the channel. We passed the now-quiet ferry slip, downtown San Diego, and were nearly abreast of Shelter Island, when the ship yawed to starboard. "Mind your helm," I hollered to the helmsman. However, when I saw my bridge indicator showed the rudder was hard to port, I stopped the screws and backed down full. When forward way was killed, we were about to leave the channel, pointed directly at dry land. Then, as suddenly as the current had taken control of the submarine, it released it. I tried to remain calm for the rest of the trek out to sea, but I believe I was silently reviewing some of the ferry pilot's cuss words.

So, the topic of this essay is - tsunami. I believe most people in the world know more about tsunami now than they did before December 26, 2004, but the impact of these phenomena are so monumental, so horrendous, that it is worth writing about. I hope you agree.

Tsunami is a Japanese word meaning harbor wave. Years ago, the term "tidal wave" was applied to these huge volumes of sea water, but it is commonly accepted now that the term is inappropriate, in that their causes are not related to weather or tides. They are caused only by geologic disturbances, primarily earthquakes, and sometimes by erupting volcanoes. They could be initiated by man-made explosions, underwater "landslides," or the untimely arrival of a large meteorite, but let's focus on the most common cause: earthquakes.

The size of a tsunami is proportional to the size of the earthquake that spawned it. An earthquake is measured and recorded by a seismograph, producing a seismogram, a visual record of the event. The instrument can measure not only the size but also the distance of the epicenter from the location of the seismograph by measuring the time delay between the primary and secondary waves. With this information, one can scribe a circle around the station after converting the time delay into distance; the epicenter lies on the circle. Using the intersecting circle from another station defines two possible locations. A third intersecting circle firmly positions the epicenter. This technique led to the establishment of the World-Wide Seismographic Station Network that contains over 120 seismographs in sixty countries.

The scale commonly used to measure the amplitude of the quake was developed by Charles Richter; it is logarithmic. Therefore, a magnitude 7 earthquake is ten times as large as a magnitude 6 event, and it releases over thirty times more energy. Scientists have found that the Richter Scale tends to saturate at measurements over 7, so a technique called moment magnitude is used to more accurately record earthquake size over magnitude 7.

To get a feel for the relative size of earthquakes, let's consider a quake that many of us (especially baseball fans tuned in to the World Series game between the Giants and Athletics) watched live on TV on October 17, 1989, the Loma Prieta quake in the San Francisco area. It did significant damage, especially to the Oakland Bay Bridge and the Marina District (where my son and his wife lived at the time). Sixty-three people died and over 3,700 were injured. That quake had a magnitude of 7.1. It doesn't even rank in the top twenty-five of earthquakes in the United States. The San Francisco quake of 1906 was magnitude 7.7; it basically wrecked the city with its destructive force and resulting fire.

The size of a tsunami is based upon several things. The release of energy is greatest in the direction normal to the fault line of the quake. As mentioned earlier, the magnitude of the geologic incident is primary in the energy released into the wave, but its size when coming ashore involves other characteristics. In most cases, it does not come ashore as a Hollywood wall of water, but rather as a tide coming in - and coming in - and coming in, extremely quickly. A gentle shallowing of the off-shore topography slows the wave, but starts the "run-up" earlier. A low-lying on-shore topography will be inundated over a very large area. In a location with a significant tidal range, the timing of the arrival of the wave is important. Arriving at high tide, the effects of tsunami and tide are additive.

Let's go back to the incident I experienced in San Diego Harbor in 1960; what caused it and what were the effects? The incident was the result of what was initially measured as an 8.6 magnitude earthquake off the coast of South-Central Chile. Subsequent analysis showed that it was much more intense. It was a 9.5 magnitude, making it the strongest earthquake ever measured. The immediate impact was a tsunami that hit the Chile-Peru coast with a wave estimated at eighty feet high; it devastated the coast. The number of deaths has never been firmly established, but could have been as many as 2000. Where else did it do damage? It hit Hilo, Hawaii with destructive force. The wave made the 10,000 kilometer journey in less than fifteen hours, making its speed across the ocean at well over 400 miles per hour. After the first wave hit, there were seven more at twelve-twenty minute intervals. The highest wave was thirty-five feet high. Sixty-one people died and 540 homes and businesses were destroyed. The tsunami continued its journey all the way to Japan, although much of its energy was gone by the time it arrived. So how did San Diego get off so easily? A tsunami travels the ocean as a high-speed, long wave-length, low amplitude wave until it "feels" bottom; then it starts to build. When it begins to build and encounters obstacles such as off-shore islands or coral reefs, energy of the system is expended before it can reach shore. Thus the effects that reached San Diego and other Southern California cities were not walls of water, but strong uncharacteristic and unpredictable currents and eddies. However Crescent City, California, just a few miles south of the Oregon border (with no off-shore islands), experienced tsunami waves of five and a half feet with minor damage.

Let's now move on to the Indian Ocean earthquake of December 26, 2004 that unleashed a tsunami that was among the deadliest disasters in modern history. It occurred just one year to the hour after a magnitude 6.6 earthquake killed an estimated 30,000 people in the city of Bam in Iran, and three days after a magnitude 8.1 quake in the Aukland Islands. In parallel with the high-profile world-wide relief efforts for those devastated by the disaster, scientists are analyzing the many aspects of the earthquake and the ensuing tsunami. This will go on for years. Initially reported at magnitude 6.8, the U.S. Geological Survey went to the moment magnitude scale and reported it at 8.1. Further analysis revised the estimate to 8.5, then 8.9, and finally to 9.0. Since that time, seismologists at Northwestern University, Seth Stein and Emile Okal, have analyzed the seismograms and found the rupture zone to be much larger than originally thought. Their analysis led to the conclusion that the quake was magnitude 9.3, not 9.0. Remembering the scale, that is a huge difference; they say the quake was three times the magnitude of the official position. The USGS is reviewing their conclusions, and have not yet revised the 9.0 figure. If the 9.3 magnitude is verified, it would make the earthquake second only in measured intensity to the Chilean event we discussed earlier.

The point of origin of the earthquake was 100 miles west of Sumatra at a depth of 18.6 miles below mean sea level. This is at the extreme western end of an earthquake belt known as the Ring of Fire, that accounts for eighty-one per cent of the world's largest earthquakes. The geographical extent of the quake is greater than I could imagine; it was of Hollywood proportions. An estimated 750 miles of fault line slipped about fifty feet in two phases. The first phase was a rupture about 250 miles long and sixty miles wide at a depth of about nineteen miles, moving at a speed of almost 4500 miles per hour for about 100 seconds. There was then a pause of about 100 seconds before the rupture proceeded northwards for the remaining 500 miles. The lateral movement was coupled by vertical movement, where the seabed is estimated to have risen several meters, triggering the powerful tsunami waves. The waves are often depicted as originating from a point source, but they actually radiated from the entire 750 miles of the rupture. They were actually observed as far away as Mexico and Chile. The energy released into the Indian Ocean has been estimated as 2.0×10 to the 18th power joules; that equates to enough energy to boil forty gallons of water for every person on earth. When I tried to picture what that rupture must have looked like, I recalled an old *New Yorker* cartoon that had a bearded man in robes on a corner holding a sign that read: "*The end is near.*"

Despite the lag of several hours between the earthquake and the arrival of the tsunami at several devastated areas, the wave was met with surprise. Unfortunately there is no tsunami warning system in the Indian Ocean. Also, the initial analysis of the quake as a magnitude 8.1 failed to alert seismologists of the actual power of the event.

In terms of loss of life, this tsunami was the most devastating in recorded history, passing the one in Awa, Japan in 1703 by a factor of more than two. When final numbers are officially assigned, it may rank as the greatest natural disaster in history. Rather than try to describe the scenes that we have all seen on television, I shall focus on results that have been realized to date. Deaths were reported from fourteen countries, with the most grim statistics coming from Indonesia where they have confirmed 130,000 deaths, but have estimated the toll could be as high as 220,000. In February, they were retrieving about 500 bodies a day. Next was Sri Lanka with 31,000 confirmed deaths, and up to 45,000 estimated. India and Thailand followed with 11,000/16,000 and 6,000/11,000 respectively. Two deaths were reported in South Africa, which is five time zones away from the earthquake. The estimates of displaced people approaches a million and a half.

The economic impact on coastal industries such as fishing is significant. For example, in Sri Lanka, the fishing industry employs about 250,000 people and is a dynamic export-oriented sector of its economy. Preliminary estimates indicate that sixty-six per cent of the fishing fleet and industrial infrastructure in the coastal regions were destroyed by the waves. Throughout the coastal regions of the Indian Ocean, efforts have been made to increase the international trade in the region. Countries have spent heavily to improve the navigability of the coastal areas, including dynamiting coral reefs in many areas. These are the same reefs that slow the progress of and suck energy from large waves. Specialists agree that death and destruction would have been less if the reefs had remained.

The environmental impact will affect the region for years to come. Forests, coastal wetlands, vegetation, rock formations, animal and plant biodiversity, ground water, etc. - all suffered massive damage. The spread of solid and liquid waste and industrial chemicals, along with the destruction of sewage collectors and treatment plants, will have predictable results. The main effect, specialists say, will come from the poisoning of fresh water supplies and the soil by salt water infiltration, depositing a salt layer over arable land.

Certainly the tourist industry was severely damaged with mass cancellations. The months following the disaster have not shown signs of recovery. Many health professionals have reported widespread psychological trauma associated with the tsunami, including the sighting of ghosts. Traditional beliefs in many of the affected regions state that a relative of the family must bury the body of the dead, or their ghost will return.

The scope of this disaster will be receiving modified definitions for years to come. From whatever standpoint I view this historic event, I still find it incomprehensible that on December 26, 2004, a quarter of a million people arose and went about their day-after-Christmas activities, completely unaware that, indeed, *the end was near.*

4.4 Where's My Oscar?

Having settled my family in a new home in Westminster, California, I drove to Long Beach to report to my first shore duty assignment as officer-in-charge, *USS Roncador* (SS-301). It would be a significant change in the pace of life from my previous three seagoing ships, a destroyer and two submarines, involving four lengthy deployments to the Western Pacific. *Roncador* was a Balao-class submarine commissioned in March 1945, then decommissioned June 1946. After spending the 1950s in mothballs, she was towed to Long Beach and established as a Reserve Training submarine. My job as OIC was to support the training and administration of two large Naval Reserve Submarine Divisions, and to maintain the submarine in good shape for training Reserves. It was winter, 1962.

In addition to the limited work space in *Roncador*, I had ample office space in the adjacent Naval Reserve Training Center, San Pedro. I fell into the relative monotony of shore duty routine rather quickly. However, I soon learned that my position made me the only easily identified and accessible submariner in the entire Los Angeles/Long Beach area. This was confirmed one day when my yeoman, YN-1(SS) Peter Roskopf, turned from his desk with a curious smile, and said, "Call for you, Captain, I think it's some dude from Hollywood." The caller identified himself as a representative from a television studio. He had a script that he wanted to discuss with a submariner. According to the plot, deep sea divers are looking for wrecks and treasure in the Philippine Sea when they encountered a sunken submarine on the bottom with its hull intact. One of the divers approaches the sub and knocks on the hull with a wrench. As he is turning away, he is startled to hear a metallic knock, apparently from inside the submarine.

The caller asks, "Is it feasible that, if the sub hadn't completely flooded, a person could have survived from 1945?"

I began mentioning the lack of air, food, etc. but interrupted myself, "What show is this for," I asked.

He replied, "The Twilight Zone."

I said, "It's perfect." Sure enough, later that year I saw the show on TV; it was excellent Rod Serling fare.

In April the following year I had a call from a large Los Angeles radio station; I had heard earlier about a submarine on the East Coast being missing. Reports that morning had been sketchy, but the radio guy had gotten later information. He said he wanted to put me on live - did I mind? Click. "I guess you know the Navy has confirmed that *Thresher* sank with all hands. Were you aware ..." I can't recall any more of the interview but a neighbor later told me he had heard it and it went fine. 129 men died in that imploding metal tube. Ever since, I have felt a special empathy for those who have just witnessed or learned of a tragic incident, and had a microphone thrust in their face for their reaction. I wonder if they remember what they said.

The major event of my final year in *Roncador* began with a phone call from a man from Universal-Review Studio. A motion picture was being shot that included a submarine sequence; they needed to ensure there were no obvious gaffs. I reported to the studio in Universal City the following morning. Being a movie buff, this was something I was looking forward to. I was introduced to the director, Ralph Nelson, who had gained acclaim the preceding year for taking on the direction of a low budget movie that others had rejected and turned it into something special. The film was *Lilies of the Field*.

I learned a few other things about the film I was to work on. Its title was *Father Goose* and it was to star Cary Grant, Leslie Caron, and Trevor Howard. Now I was really excited about the opportunity to participate (in a small way) in the filming of a major motion picture. I was particularly happy to find that I would see Cary Grant and Trevor Howard work together in a scene. However, I was sad to learn that all scenes that included Leslie Caron were "in the can." I also learned that Ralph Nelson was not the original director; he had been hired when the picture was clearly going over budget in time and cost and had some other serious problems. What a good move it was to bring in Ralph Nelson.

We went right to work on the set of a submarine conning tower, rigged for night vision, where the scene was going be a torpedo run on a Japanese ship. As soon as I had been introduced to the actors in their Navy uniforms (these were just bit parts in the movie) I noted they all were wearing their dolphins on the wrong side. While they were changing, I mentioned that the night vision was retained by using red lights in the conning tower; they had blue ones. One of the old prop men grunted, "When I was in the boats in '32, we used blue." He went out to get the red light lenses; man, I was on a roll. Soon after, the actors went through a dry run of the script. To my amusement, I noticed that these actors had the relevant pages of the script open but out of sight of the camera and the director. They hadn't memorized their lines, I concluded. Hmmm ... I thought - I could do that. If one of them got sick, I could easily step in and take the part. I could picture a movie magazine headline: *Navy Guy Steals Show From Cary Grant*. Didn't happen. Oh well, I digress. On with the dry run. At the end of the torpedo run, the "captain" yelled "Fire!" The Director looked at me, and I told him the script, as written, was not the dialogue that would be used in that type of torpedo run, and the captain would never yell "fire" in a submerged submarine unless he saw one. We went back to the office and met the Producer, Robert Arthur; Mr. Nelson said we need to write some script. I started to feel that perhaps I was being too picky, and suggested the only audience that would recognize the flaws in the dialogue would be other submariners. Director looked at producer who said, "Let's get it right." We went back to the office where we met Producer Robert Arthur. Mr. Nelson told him we needed to write some script. So, we wrote some script. At this point, I was amazed at how professional and flexible these gentlemen were.

Since the locale of the picture was on islands in the Western Pacific, the on-location shots were being done in Jamaica, and the daily shots were flown to the studio for review. I was invited to join the producer and director to examine the location shots of the previous day. I was really impressed that the producer spotted an error: the stand-in for Cary Grant was wearing the wrong color shirt (he only had two shirts in the movie) in a scene being reviewed. Considering that the scenes were not shot in sequence, spotting that kind of error meant he really had the entire motion picture in his head. That blew my concept of producers out of the water. I thought they stayed in big offices, behind big desks, calling everyone "Baby" and giving private "screen tests" to beautiful starlets. Robert Arthur did not fit that mold at all. He was a professional.

The next day, the schedule called for shooting the external shots of the submarine surfacing. We didn't go to the waterfront; rather we walked to a building that may have been a large aircraft hangar. Near the middle of it was the superstructure of a submarine mounted on a platform with wheels. Toward one end of the building was the camera set up for shooting the scene. Behind the "submarine" was a very large translucent screen; far behind the screen was a motion picture projector. While I was looking around and getting the picture of how the shooting would be done, I glanced to the side of the building where I was standing; I'm sure my jaw dropped. I asked a prop guy nearby, "Is that the original *Phantom of the Opera* set?"

"Yup, that's it," he answered.

Suddenly, I felt that I was in the midst of filmdom history. How many movies had I seen, I wondered, that contained scenes shot right where I was standing? As they were about to start shooting, the projector was turned on, and a sea scene was projected on the see-through screen behind the "submarine," so from the camera's vantage point, the "submarine" appeared to be in the ocean. The horizon rocked with a gentle motion; I realized that when we viewed the shot, the horizon would be still and the ship would appear to be rocking. In the scene, the sub had just surfaced and the captain emerged from the conning tower hatch to the bridge. To make it more realistic, water should have been splashing around. Two prop guys were standing on the hangar floor throwing buckets of water against the sub's side. That, I thought, was really rinky-dink. Did it work? Well, you'll have to see the movie and judge for yourself.

The next day we had a scene where Cary Grant was engaged in a radio conversation with Trevor Howard and, although in the movie they were many miles from each other, their sets were adjacent so the timing was easy; they could actually hear each other speaking. It was fascinating watching two pros like Cary Grant and Trevor Howard play off one another - but I noted the wisdom of Ralph Nelson. He knew the talent he was dealing with and he let them make the interactions work. As the scene was finishing, I heard someone holler, "Trevor!"

Trevor turned and called, "Sonny!" There, walking onto the set was a very big, very red-faced Sonny Tufts. Apparently they were old drinking buddies and hadn't seen each other for quite a while. As I watched that scene unfold, I thought, *This is fun*!

Later, I was talking with Ralph Nelson and a couple of others, and we were naming movies with Cary Grant and submarines in them. They were trying to figure whether Cary Grant had more time in subs than I did. The movie that nearly all of them enjoyed the most was *Operation Petticoat*. There were only two who had not seen the movie: I was one, Ralph Nelson was the other. In another discussion with the director, I asked him what his hopes were for the picture. He was optimistic as he explained that there were months of hard work ahead in the splicing and cutting of film to ensure a smooth flow and a well-told story. However, if finished in time, he hoped it might be picked to be the Christmas show at Radio City Music Hall.

As my time on the project was winding down, Ralph Nelson made a very generous offer and I jumped on it. It was for an outing the following Saturday. Pete and Nuana Roskopf and Evelyn and I arrived at the Universal-Review Studios Saturday afternoon where Mr. Nelson had set up a tour of the lot for us. We saw many familiar sets on the tour, but the only one I specifically recall is *Gilligan's Island*. After the tour we went to a Chinese restaurant nearby where we met with Ralph Nelson; he treated us to dinner. Then we returned to the studio and entered the review room that I had been in days earlier. The chairs were heavily padded with an ash tray built into the arm of each. Being a smoker then, I appreciated that feature. The projectionist was ready; we sat back, relaxed, and enjoyed our private showing of *Operation Petticoat*. A delightful evening.

A month or so later, I had orders to be navigator in *USS Tench* in Groton, Connecticut. We hustled across country so I could be read into the security aspects of a cruise I would be leaving on in days. It was one of those cruises where we'd disappear from sight, unable to communicate, then reappear somewhere in the North Atlantic months later. Returning before Christmas, I found that *Father Goose* was indeed selected to be the Christmas Show at Radio City. Evelyn and I decided to drive to New York and see it during Christmas week. We took the harrowing drive into New York City to Radio City and, upon arrival, noted that the line to get in was at least two blocks long; the wait would be hours. Reluctantly, we decided to turn around and go home.

Then, Navy life got in the way, and I didn't see the movie until a few years later - aboard ship. I read the promotional pamphlet that came with the movie and learned for the first time that *Father Goose* had won one Academy Award - for screenplay. So the Academy had liked the script. Wait a minute, I wrote a part of that script. Hey! Where's my Oscar?

4.5 The Risks of Success

The late summer California sun was low in the sky as I maneuvered my '64 Chevy wagon into the garage and entered the house through the sliding glass door.

"Honey, I'm home. We're heading East!"

"We're what?"

"We are going back to the East Coast. I have orders to report as third officer of *USS Tench* in New London."

And so began another submarine adventure in a different environment. I was familiar with New London, having attended the six-month basic submarine course several years before. But my sea duty to date had been aboard a destroyer and two submarines, *Razorback* and *Pomodon*, all based in San Diego. I was a Pacific Ocean sailor. That would now change.

That evening I received a phone call from LCDR Jim Morrison (made-up name), Commanding Officer of *Tench* to verify that I had received my orders. He informed me that *Tench* would be leaving on an important deployment next month and there was much to be done in preparation. I would be navigator and needed to have my clearances upgraded and accomplish a number of tasks that he could not address over the phone. He convinced me I was needed as soon as possible and not to add leave to my travel time. I accelerated the turn-over of my current job as officer-in-charge of the reserve training submarine, *Roncador*, sold our home, packed the Chevy, and headed East with my wife and three tots.

After checking in at Naval Submarine Base, New London and boarding *Tench*, I filled out loads of paperwork. Clearances were accelerated and I was read in on the forthcoming deployment. It was a highly-classified operation in which I could easily see what a challenge I would have as navigator. I quickly realized that all the training on how to turn a submarine into a destructive war machine, efficient at hunting and killing surface ships and other submarines, was for naught. On this mission, *Tench* would be a 307-foot long SPY. Remember, this was the mid-1960's: the peak of the Cold War.

With Evelyn and the children situated in a small rental home in Ledyard, I bid farewell and proceeded to board *Tench* at the base, taking my navigator's station in the conning tower. We quietly slipped into the Thames River heading south to Long Island Sound, Block Island Sound, Narragansett Bay, and on to the open Atlantic. The first day at sea on an extended cruise is normally a somber time with the crew reflecting on what they left behind, while not knowing what lies ahead. With the type of mission we had, they actually did not know where we were going nor what we would do there. The crew had confidence in their skipper; LCDR Morrison was a large, rather imposing figure with a very direct nature. He expected a lot from his crew and did not tolerate incompetence. He left no doubt who was in charge.

The third day out, the captain spent an unusual amount of time in the radio shack; it was clear that something was up. Later in the afternoon, he called for the exec and me to come to his cabin. He said to me, "We have had a temporary change of plans; I want you plot a course for Terceira Island in the Azores and let me know when we can arrive there assuming the same speed of advance we are currently using. After I get that information, I'll brief you and the other officers on what's up."

After doing as told, I briefed the captain on the time to reach Terceira. He gathered the officers and the chief-of-the-boat (COB) in the ward room and said, "What I am about to tell you is not to reach the ears of any crew member until I release the information. Is that clear?"

"Yes, sir," was the unanimous reply.

"I have just changed our course to head for the Azores. One of our crew members has experienced a tragedy. We all know how proud MM1 Thompson is of his large family. Yesterday, his house burned down, and four of his five children died in the blaze." The news was greeted with gasps. The captain continued, "I don't plan to tell him, or anyone, until just before we arrive at Terceira Island where a plane will be waiting to fly him back home. COMSUBLANT is making the arrangements; the division and squadron staffs are doing their best to care for his wife and surviving child. There's little we can do except pray for Thompson and his wife."

Submarines are known for having close-knit crews and this is especially true of subs on cruise where the same eighty men will live in a metal tube for months at a time. Needless to say, Thompson's departure was an emotional one. The remainder of our transit to Plymouth, England was even more somber than earlier.

The stay in Plymouth was short, topping off fuel, water, and a few other supplies. We left after dark and proceeded east in the English Channel, through the buoy Straits of Dover, and north into the foggy North Sea. When well clear of land and in low visibility, *Tench* submerged. Thus began our classified movement where we were to remain undetected by any source until well after our mission was complete. Our transit north into the Norwegian Sea, well off the coast of Norway, was done submerged, snorkeling whenever feasible. We had a system installed called Prairie-Masker that emitted an envelope of bubbles around the hull while snorkeling that limited and changed the characteristics of the sound we made with the engines running. Even if the sound were detected by a passive sonar, it would be quite difficult to classify as a snorkeling submarine.

Eventually, when we were north of North Cape (the northernmost point of Europe) we turned east into the Barents Sea. This body extends from the ice cap to the northern coast of Russia. The Soviets considered it their operating area; however, for the next few weeks, this would be our patrol area. The hazards of being detected in the Barents were obvious. Our mission was to locate, detect, classify, and record electronic emissions with the special equipment we had aboard. The analysis would be primarily done by a "guest" we had aboard who was an expert in acquiring and analyzing this type of intelligence; he also spoke Russian.

Soon after arriving in the Barents, the COB informed the captain that our "guest" had been experiencing physical problems during the transit up the coast, and appeared to be in considerable pain. The problem seemed to be hemorrhoids. "He'd better be ready to do his job or we could be wasting our time!" The captain was clearly not impressed. However, in the following days the situation grew worse. With his bunk in the After Torpedo Room (where there is a head), his morning sessions in the head were accompanied with screams of pain. The morale of the other sailors bunking in that compartment was dropping rapidly. The hospital corpsman did what he could to ease the pain, but it did little good. His condition continued to worsen.

The next day, the captain called a meeting of the department heads, the COB, and the corpsman. He had the corpsman outline the physical condition of his patient and assess the seriousness of his condition. The COB said a few words about the negative effects the situation had on the morale of the crew. I mentioned that if we were to leave station today, it would be the better part of a week before we could get the needed medical attention. The exec added that the quality of intelligence we acquired wouldn't be the same without his services. I believe the captain closed the meeting with a resounding, "Oh, shit" and stomped out.

I was never close with Captain Morrison, but I could feel the pain he was experiencing, knowing what he had to do. He conferred a while with the exec, then told me to plot a track to Holy Loch, Scotland. The exec told the conning officer what we were doing. The captain made the announcement to the crew.

The journey back down the Norwegian coast was long and quiet; it was still a classified movement. Approaching Scotland the captain broke radio silence to announce our arrival before entering the Firth of Clyde, alert the tender in Holy Loch of our wish to deliver our patient to their medical staff, and, oh yes, tell COMSUBLANT that *Tench* was not in the Barents Sea, but off the coast of Scotland. This, of course, was painful for the captain, and his request to return to our patrol assignment was denied. Considering the time it took to get to Scotland and the time it would take to get back - and without an intelligence specialist aboard would not have made good sense to send *Tench* back to complete our patrol. Our mission was not accomplished, but was over.

As we proceeded up the Clyde the visibility was poor, the tide was ebbing, and radar images were not familiar. We moved cautiously. I was in a state of high anxiety; with no visual positioning available, shaky radar ranging, and tidal effects, we went buoy to buoy. What an inglorious punctuation to our cruise it would be to go aground in Scotland!

To my relief, the fog lifted enough to get a visual fix. We spotted a small craft making good speed toward us. Because *Tench* had not had prior authorization to enter Scotland, the captain had radioed local authorities that we had a medical emergency aboard, and were headed to the submarine base at Holy Loch. The locals responded to this as you hope friendly countries would: they dispatched an official with a medical team to relieve us of our emergency and get him into the hospital as quickly as possible. Whoops! Another dilemma. If surgery would be required to relieve the situation, a man with the clearances our intelligence specialist had could not be put under anesthetics without one with similar clearance present. The captain could not get into the details of why he couldn't accept their offer, but he thanked them and proceeded toward Holy Loch.

The rest of the journey up the Loch went without incident and the patient was delivered to the medical staff of the *Tender*, who surgically repaired the damaged afterquarters of the patient. However, the next morning, the local papers blazed with headlines: *United States Submarine Tench Rejects Local Medical Assistance for Seriously Ill Sailor.*

The voyage back to New London went without incident. I used the time to complete my Qualification for Command thesis that I knew very few people would ever read it: Navigating for a Patrol in the Barents Sea. After returning home and no longer needing access to the information for this mission, that clearance was removed, appropriately. I found it amusing that I no longer could have access to my own thesis.

So, my tale of the cruise ends, but there is a little more to my story. I didn't follow the career of Jim Morrison after that; as I mentioned, I never felt particularly close to him. I went on to an executive officer tour and then to shore duty at the Office of Naval Research. At some point I ran across Jim Morrison's name and felt like I had taken a body blow. It read: "LCDR James Morrison, USN (Ret.)." At a period when diesel-electric submarine commands were diminishing, being selected to command one reflected career success, and selection of your command for a patrol reflected considerable confidence in your capabilities. Jim Morrison was clearly headed for bigger things in his career, until the *Tench* patrol. He was not selected for promotion to commander after completing a tour commanding a submarine. No collision, no grounding, no insurrection aboard, no insubordination, but an incomplete patrol assignment. Never had the risks that accompany success come into clearer focus.

4.6 Just Getting There Was Half the Fun

It was a rather gloomy fall morning when we drove from our home in Groton, across the bridge over the Thames, to the tender in New London where USS *Halfbeak* was berthed. Another deployment was to begin at 8 o'clock, this one to the Mediterranean. Normally I would look forward to another adventure, but this was the fifth multi-month deployment in the two years since I drove Evelyn and our three little ones across our beautiful land from the sunny climes of Southern California. I felt a lot of guilt about leaving Evelyn once more to face a Connecticut winter with three small children. But, that's what I did for a living. LCDR Arthur Stanley Moreau, Jr. was the commanding officer; I was his executive officer.

After backing clear of the submarine tender, the officer of the deck eased *Halfbeak* into the safe channel of the Thames, heading south toward Long Island Sound, and thence through Block Island Sound, around Montauk Point to the broad Atlantic Ocean. The first day of a deployment is usually quiet, with the crew rather subdued as they get back to the routines of at-sea life during the boring ocean transit, wondering what adventures lie ahead.

The third day out, we were in the Gulf Stream; the weather and the water were warm and pleasant. The captain announced Swim Call, and we manned our stations. The OD killed the way; the Chief of the Boat, Master Chief Andy Anderson, was in charge of keeping things safe on deck. I stationed myself on the bridge as a safety observer with the ship's sharpshooter alongside, with his M-1 rifle and a full clip. After about a half hour, I announced the end of the swim. As the swimmers climbed aboard, the captain appeared on deck in swim trunks and goggles. He called up to me that he was going to jump in and do a visual inspection of the sonar dome. I resisted telling him what a weird idea I thought that was, and over the side he went. He swam to the bow, took a few deep breaths, and plunged. Less than five seconds later, the port lookout called, "Shark!"

The OD responded, "Holy shit!" The shark was thirty yards off the port beam and not approaching; the sharpshooter raised his rifle to sight in. I directed him not to shoot unless I said to and had the lookouts scan the waters to see if any others were around.

We waited several nervous seconds until the captain reappeared. As his head bobbed to the surface, the COB gestured and shouted, "Shark!" The skipper fairly flew to the ladder and onto the deck. The 1MC announced, "Now secure from swim call; rig ship for dive." The incident was over; the transit continued.

Two days later, we scheduled some diving officer training, spreading the word through the boat so men wouldn't be alarmed with sudden angles. It also serves as a warning to secure anything loose that might become a missile hazard. We initially went to periscope depth, fifty-eight feet at the keel. The captain took the conn and began running the training; he seemed to take great joy in turning this twenty-four year old submarine into a slow-moving roller coaster. I always position myself in the control room; it is just below the conning tower and above the pump room. That is where the diving officer positions himself, just behind the bow and stern operator. They are on the port side. Behind the diving officer, on the starboard side is the air manifold operator. These are all critical stations while the submarine is submerged. In qualifying for submarines, I had learned how to operate all of these stations in routine situations and in emergencies. That is why I stationed myself there while the captain was teasing the diving officers into using larger angles to change depth.

Consider a few numbers: our test depth was 412 feet; we seldom operated below 250 feet keel depth; the depth sensor was just forward of amidships; the submarine was 306 feet in length. If you pass 200 feet with a down angle of fifteen degrees, what is the depth of the bow? That may seem like an innocent academic question, but on this day, on this dive, that is where we were when we heard a loud pop followed by the whoosh of flooding water, then thwack, like a rifle shot in the control room. "All stop - all back full" called the captain, "Get me up!"

Already the diving officer had ordered full rise on both planes and called, "Shut the vents" to the hydraulic manifold operator. "Blow bow buoyancy," the diving officer called to the air manifold operator; then "blow main ballast."

Quickly the angle changed to an up angle; the captain ordered, "All stop, all ahead full." As we careened upward, I told the diving officer, "Don't use the blower." We broke the surface with a significant up angle, then the bow came slamming down as we leveled off. "All stop," the captain ordered. The emergency was over. Let me interrupt the story to provide a bit of explanation so the casualty and the actions will make sense. A submarine submerges by flooding its ballast tanks that are located outside the pressure hull and are open to the sea at the bottom. At the top are large lines that lead to vent valves. Water cannot enter these tanks unless the air in the tank is vacated. When the vents are opened by the hydraulic manifold operator, the air escapes, the tanks flood quickly, and the sub goes beneath the surface. To surface, the vents are shut, and 600-pound air is fed into the tanks to blow the water out the open ports at the base. However, as the sub breaks the surface, the compressed air is preserved by starting the low pressure blower (located in the pump room) that delivers large volumes of air at 10 psi through the blower manifold, located in the control room. This removes residual water from the ballast tanks. The low-pressure blower lines are six inches in diameter. The manifold (and the submarine) are protected by flapper valves that serve as check valves, that is, they permit only one-way flow.

To continue, "What happened?" the captain asked as I climbed to the conning tower. I responded, "I believe a low pressure blower line failed and the water rushed through the line and slammed into the blower manifold, and the check valve held. I'd like to go topside with Andy and see if we can locate the failure." The chief and I went to the bridge, then down on deck. Opening a deck access section we lowered ourselves onto the pressure hull near where the low pressure lines accessed the hull. The first one we examined was the culprit; a pressure-induced hole was obvious. What wasn't obvious was why it failed now but not on the deep test dive after the last overhaul.

The engineer officer, the COB, the captain, and I met in the wardroom to consider our options. For the captain, this was big. A submarine that cannot submerge cannot complete missions and should not be at sea. If he were to be ordered to return to port, another submarine would be sent to sea on short notice to replace *Halfbeak*. Unfair as it may sound, the very promising career of Art Moreau would suffer a heavy hit. Never mind the cause, he would be known as the skipper whose submarine couldn't complete its mission. Art Moreau would not let that happen to his ship and crew.

"Do you have 3-M repair products on board?" I asked the engineer.

"The epoxy stuff and glass wrap? Yes."

I said, "captain, I had experience using this material when I was engineer officer aboard *Pomodon*. It is incredibly strong. I'd like to try a temporary repair."

"Did you use it where it is exposed to the sea under pressure?" he asked.

"No sir." He was silent, staring off into space.

He got up. "Do it," he said and went to his stateroom.

An engineman and an electrician, both of whom had used the product (but not for this purpose), reviewed the instructions with me. We discussed the best way to adapt it to this purpose. When we reached agreement, we went topside and made the repair. Upon completion, I reported to the captain the time needed for the material to cure and set. We continued our transit on the surface that night. In the morning I reported that the repair appeared to be complete. He went topside with me to inspect the work. It looked like an over-zealous mother's bandage of a skinned knee.

He felt it, knocked on it, then smiled and said, "Let's go."

Once below, the captain said, "Prepare the ship to dive. I want the engineer (who was the ship's diving officer) on the dive." This was vintage Art Moreau. He would not live with demons; he would fearlessly face them down, then move on to the next one.

"Dive, dive" came over the 1MC, "Make your depth 58 feet" the captain called to the diving officer. The dive was routine. After a few minutes at periscope depth, he ordered, "Make your depth 100 feet." I put on a casual calm as we descended; fortunately, no one could measure my heart rate or blood pressure. When the depth gauge read 100, and nothing untoward occurred, I began to breathe easier. "One-five-zero feet" came from the conning tower. Down we went, slowly, with a gentle angle. Eventually we arrived at that depth, and nothing happened. After a few minutes, the Captain returned to 100 feet, took a good sonar sweep, and ascended to periscope depth. After surfacing, he set the regular watch and we continued the transit. When we met in the passageway of the forward battery compartment, Captain Moreau said, "Tell all diving and conning officers that I am restricting our depth to a maximum of one hundred fifty feet for the remainder of the transit."

I replied "Aye, captain," then asked, "You didn't report this, did you?" With a sly smile, he ducked behind the curtain to his stateroom without answering. The ocean crossing ended at Rota, Spain, where we moored alongside the submarine tender. The first one off the ship was the captain to call on a friend who was the repair officer on the *Tender*. From here on, I have nothing to report first hand, but I surmise that the Captain first was assured that the *Tender* could make permanent repairs to our problem before a formal report was made. Delays in reporting such a casualty would have cost many commanding officers their commands, but the aggressive (and successful) way this was handled resulted in no punitive action. In fact, I think it just enhanced his reputation.

Art Moreau succeeded in all the positions he held, but not through caution or even by following all the rules. He was a throwback to the World War II submarine skippers who amazed the Navy with their exploits and their successes; he lived on the edge.

Many years later, when the Iran-Contra incident broke, it was no surprise to me to learn that the NATO commander for Eastern Europe and Commander, Naval Forces, Mediterranean was 4-star Admiral, Arthur Stanley Moreau, Jr. To this day, I have to believe that he was in on it; it was the type of secret operation he would have loved. However, on December 8, 1986, in Naples, he suffered a heart attack and died - at age fifty-five, leaving his wife Katie and 5 children. What a loss!

But, I digress. Repairs were completed in Rota, and, once again *Halfbeak* put to sea and headed south to continue our deployment, despite its rather tenuous beginning, toward the business end of our cruise: the Med. I could continue with tales of our adventures in Gibralter, Naples, San Remo, Villafranche, Monte Carlo, Majorca, Crete, and the rest of that memorable cruise, but, well, some other time. Besides, as I mentioned at the outset, just getting there was half the fun.

Word-of-mouth is crucial for any author to succeed.
If you enjoyed this book, please leave a review online.
Even if it's just a sentence or two.
It would make all the difference and is very much appreciated.

High Tide Publications, Inc.

Edward W. Lull

Poet and Essayist

Edward Lull was born in Pennsylvania and grew up in Upstate New York. He graduated from the U.S. Naval Academy in the Class of 1955. His first career was as a Naval Officer with duty primarily in submarines. He earned a masters degree from The George Washington University in 1969. He retired from the Navy as Commander, USN in 1975.

After retirement from the Navy, in his second career he served in management and executive positions in small hi-tech companies in the Washington, D.C. area. His final position was President and Chairman of the Board of a non-profit company, The Professional Group, sponsored by The George Mason University.

Ed began a third career as a writer at age 65. He is a former member of the Williamsburg Poetry Guild and The Williamsburg Poetry Workshop. He taught a Beginning Poetry Workshop for the Christopher Wren Association for three years. In 2008, he founded the poetry workshop, James City Poets, that continues operating today.

In 1999, Ed joined the Poetry Society of Virginia and served four terms as its President and ten years as an Executive Director. He initiated the Poetry in the Schools program, working with Virginia Association of Teachers of English (V.A.T.E.) to promote the study of poetry, both reading and writing, in Virginia's schools. Ed attended and presented poetry programs at the annual V.A.T.E. Conference and presented poetry programs to numerous secondary schools throughout the Commonwealth. In 2012, Ed was presented the inaugural Emyl Jenkins Award "... for inspiring a love of writing and writing education in Virginia."

In 2002, Ed began a monthly program of poetry readings by invited poets on the first Saturday of the month; the Saturday Poetry Series is in its 18th year. Ed brought the Annual Poetry Festival to Williamsburg in 2001 and ran it for 16 years. When the one-day Williamsburg Book Festival was established as part of the Occasion for the Arts, Ed negotiated to have a poetry program as part of the Festival. He schedules and emcees that program annually in October.

Ed joined The Emerson Society of Virginia in 2002 and has maintained continuous membership since. Members have dinner meetings monthly followed by a designated member presenting an essay. He served as President of the organization from 2008 to 2018.

Ed maintains Life Memberships in The Poetry Society of Virginia, The U. S. Naval Institute, The U. S. Naval Academy Alumni Association, and the Military Officers Association.

Edward Lull's writing and editing credits are listed separately.

Edward W. Lull

List of Publications

Books Published:

2003   *Cabin Boy to Captain: A Sea Story* - Morris Publishing, Kearney, NE - A historical novel set in 16th Century Elizabethan England; written in Blank Verse

2005   *Where Giants Walked* - Infinity Publishing, West Conshohocken, PA - A compendium of poems in 5 parts: Ballads, Stories, Light Verse, Reflections, Impressions

2007   *The Sailors: Birth of a Navy* - Infinity Publishing, West Conshohocken, PA - Twelve narrative poems relating key events of the early Navy, 1776-1815

2011   *Bits and Pieces: A Memoir* - Infinity Publishing, West Conshohocken, PA - A series of poems and essays that document incidents in the life of the author

2013   *Creating Form Poetry: A Poet's Handbook* - Infinity Publishing, West Conshohocken,PA - A how-to book that provides instructions for writing and examples of 34 poetry forms

2017   *The Reality and Fantasy of MY WORLD* - High Tide Publications, Inc., Deltaville, VA - An anthology of poems that focus on days of celebration and remembrance and life experiences of the author

Editor Credits:

2000   *Vinyage Wine and Good Spirits - The Williamsburg Poetry Guild toasts the 20th Century* -Editor: Edward W. Lull

2006   *Four Virginia Poets Laureate: A Teaching Guide* - Features poetry and bios of the Virginia Poets Laureate from 1996-2004. Also included are critical reviews of their work and Classroom exercises. Editors: Carolyn Kreiter-Foronda and Edward W. Lull

2013 - *Distant Horizons: As Seen by Williamsburg Poets* - An anthology of poems by the Williamsburg Poetry Workshop and the James City Poets. Editors: Ron Landa and Edward W. Lull

2018   *ESSAYS By The Emerson Society of Williamsburg*, Volumes 1 thru 9. Editor: Edward W. Lull

www.ingramcontent.com/pod-product-compliance
Lightning Source LLC
Chambersburg PA
CBHW071127150426
42813CB00075BA/3476/J